RETURN FROM
EXTINCTION

The Triumph of the Elephant Seal

LINDA L. RICHARDS

ORCA BOOK PUBLISHERS

Published in Canada and the United States
in 2020 by Orca Book Publishers.
orcabook.com

Library and Archives Canada Cataloguing in Publication
Title: Return from extinction: the triumph of
the elephant seal / Linda L. Richards.
Names: Richards, Linda L. (Linda Lea), 1960– author.
Series: Orca wild.
Description: Series statement: Orca wild | Includes
bibliographical references and index.
Identifiers: Canadiana (print) 20200186000 | Canadiana
(ebook) 20200186019 | ISBN 9781459821361 (hardcover) |
ISBN 9781459821378 (PDF) | ISBN 9781459821385 (EPUB)
Subjects: LCSH: Northern elephant seal—Juvenile literature.
Classification: LCC QL737.P64 R53 2020 | DDC j599.79/4—dc23

Library of Congress Control Number: 2020931815

Summary: This nonfiction book for middle readers tells the
story of the northern elephant seal, from being hunted to near
extinction less than 100 years ago to their thriving population of
more than 250,000 today. Illustrated with photos from the author.

Orca Book Publishers is committed to reducing
the consumption of nonrenewable resources in the
making of our books. We make every effort to use
materials that support a sustainable future.

Orca Book Publishers gratefully acknowledges the support
for its publishing programs provided by the following
agencies: the Government of Canada, the Canada Council
for the Arts and the Province of British Columbia through
the BC Arts Council and the Book Publishing Tax Credit.

Front cover photos by Winfried Wisniewski/Getty Images
and Ai Angel Gentel/Getty Images
Back cover photo by Xavier Hoenner
/ 500px/Getty Images
Design by Dahlia Yuen

Printed and bound in China.

23 22 21 20 • 1 2 3 4

Looking down at the northern elephant seal rookery at
Piedras Blancas in California. At certain times of the
year, you can't see anything but elephant seals when
you take in this view. They are packed in like sardines!
LINDA L. RICHARDS

"Unless someone like you cares a whole awful lot,
nothing is going to get better.
It's not."
—Dr. Seuss, *The Lorax*

CONTENTS

INTRODUCTION   1

1
MEET THE ELEPHANT SEAL

My, What a Big Nose You Have!   5
Southern Cousins   9
A Life at Sea   10
Speed and Grace   11
Doctor Jekyll and Mister Dive   12
Size Matters   15
My, What Big Eyes You Have!   15
Elephant Seals Have Good Hearing!   16
Home Sweet Home   18
The Politics of the Rookery   20

2
THE ELEPHANT SEAL THROUGH THE AGES

The Elephant Seal in Prehistory   25
How Did They End Up Looking Like *That*?   26
Enaliarctos   28
Hunted to Extinction   28
Science and Protection   34
Champions of Adaptation   36
Happy Endings   39
Modern Breeding Grounds   39

2
THE CYCLE OF LIFE

A Year in the Life of an Elephant Seal   43
A Catastrophic Molt   47
Shiny and New   48
Hunting and Foraging   53
Meet the Family   56
Fasting on the Beach   59
What and Who Eats *Them*?   61

3
THE ELEPHANT SEAL TODAY

Garbage in the Ocean   63
Warming Waters   64
Science and the Seal   64
Where and How to See Them   68
Point Reyes   71
Marine Mammal Center   71
Race Rocks   72
Along the Coast   73
Environmental Challenges   73
Climate Change   76
Genetic Challenges   77
A Good-News Story   80

GLOSSARY   82

RESOURCES   84

ACKNOWLEDGMENTS   86

INDEX   88

The boardwalk at Piedras Blancas near San Simeon, CA, offers a clear view of the elephant seals going about their business. There is free parking nearby, and you can view the seals at all times of the year.
LINDA L RICHARDS

INTRODUCTION

I could not have imagined the powerful impression they would make on me.

I was traveling in the area, and people were telling me all the sights I needed to be sure to see. It's California's Central Coast, so there are a lot of sights like that. The charming village of Cambria. The old Hollywood nuttiness of Hearst Castle. The elephant seals. Big Sur. Moonstone Beach. The…wait, wait…back up. Elephant seals?

No, really. Everyone I talked to said the same thing. *You have to see them.*

I *had* to.

I really couldn't imagine why. Lots of seals. Big deal. Kind of weird-looking even. Not super cute like the harbor seals I would sometimes see near my home in British Columbia. And it wasn't like you could pet them or anything. Or feed them. Or even get super close. Why would I take the time? I didn't have anything against seals. But there is an actual *castle* right across the street that takes hours to tour. There's also a cute roadside restaurant that advertises the best burgers *in the world.*

So visiting the seals wasn't anywhere near the top of my list. And then I forgot about them as I prepared to make my way north toward Monterey and San Francisco via Big Sur.

On that drive a highway sign caught my eye. It read, *Vista Point: Elephant Seal Viewing Area.* I decided I'd stop and have a quick peek. Five minutes. Back on the road in a heartbeat.

I parked the car. I walked a few feet to a boardwalk 5 miles (just over 8 kilometers) long, elevated above the ocean, and looked down. The beach below me was full. At first I thought I was seeing hundreds of dead creatures.

Flipper to flipper and tail to tail. The number of elephant seals you'll see at one time depends entirely on what time of the year you visit. In certain months there is no place you can look and *not* see a lot of seals doing something—or a lot of seals doing very little.
LINDA L. RICHARDS

Then I looked more closely and saw that the beach was teeming with life.

They were flipper to flipper and tail to tail. They were lying on the beach companionably, flipping sand, and they seemed to be having seal conversations.

That first visit I was intrigued. My trip up the coast got delayed by a whole day as I stayed and lingered and began to learn. There are *docents* at the Piedras Blancas elephant seal *rookery*. They volunteer many hours helping the thousands of visitors who come every year to learn about the seals.

And so I pestered the docents, one after another, asking questions. Every answer I got seemed to give birth to more questions. The spectacle here on the beach near Hearst Castle? This was pretty new, they told me. Not so many years ago, there were no seals on the beach at Piedras Blancas. Not so many years before that there were only 20 to 70 northern elephant seals left in their entire range.

I looked out at the hundreds and hundreds of seals on the beach at that moment. I listened to their honky voices and breathed in their farmyard-type smells and wondered how this had happened. How had this miracle occurred? And when I started to get answers, it dawned on me that it really was, in fact, sort of a miracle. A good-news story in a world where it sometimes seems we hear too much bad news. It was a story filled with wild coincidences and narrow misses and also the helping hands of a few good people with the right idea. Everything had come together in just the right way, and the realization of that made my heart sing. It also made me realize it was a story I wanted to share with you.

And so here we are.

Young males sparring in shallow water just offshore are a common sight at most elephant seal rookeries. Like youngsters everywhere, these males are using play to learn the skills they will need as adults.
LINDA L. RICHARDS

The mature male northern elephant seal has the well-developed proboscis that gives this species its name. Does he look like an elephant? Not really, right? And he uses his proboscis very differently than an elephant might. Still, you can't help but be reminded of the land animal called elephant when you look at one of these guys.

1
MEET THE ELEPHANT SEAL

MY, WHAT A BIG NOSE YOU HAVE!

You don't forget the first time you see an adult male elephant seal. Imagine a creature the size of a small bus, making sounds as loud as an airplane taking off and moving inelegantly—though not always slowly—across the sand.

Though they look something like the land-based creatures that gave them their name, elephant seals are not related to elephants. Elephant seals can be the same color as elephants. And the nose of the male elephant seal is distinctively large and mobile, but that's where the similarities end.

The elephant seal gets its name from the trunk-like *proboscis* that mature males have. A proboscis is a flexible snout found in this seal species, elephants and some insects.

You can tell male and female elephant seals apart at a glance. Aside from being *so much* larger than females, males also have a very noticeable proboscis. (That's the noselike thing on their faces. It gives them sort of a comical look. To us, I mean. They probably think they look very handsome.) LINDA L. RICHARDS

Annoyingly, even scientists can't agree on the pronunciation of the word, so don't sweat it if you feel like you might not get it right. Some people say *pro-boss-us* and others pronounce the *C* as hard: *pro-boss-kus*. But if you just say *nose* everyone will know what you mean anyway.

Only mature male elephant seals have a nose big enough to be called a proboscis, which makes it easy to tell the adults from the juveniles. Females—who are always much, much smaller than the males—have that sweet face everyone always thinks of right away when someone says the word *seal*. They have large eyes, a smooth head and a friendly expression.

As far as scientists can tell, the purpose of the nose is all about breeding. The bigger the nose, the more awesome, impressive and scary sounds the male can make. This scares off smaller (and probably less noisy) competitors when establishing their territories.

The sound is distinctive and also hard to describe. Some people say the sound is like a drum. Others say it sounds like zombies. But since I've never actually *heard* a zombie, I can't say one way or the other. The part the proboscis plays in making the sound is unclear, but it does seem to play a part. The sound is made in the throat, larynx and chest. It resonates in the nasal chamber but isn't produced in there.

However the sounds are made, they are so distinctive that seals remember them from year to year. If a high-status male has chased away his rivals, in later years those rivals will remember his vocalizations and stay away.

To put that another way, researchers have observed that elephant seals can recognize each other's voices, even after long periods without hearing them.

READY FOR MY CLOSEUP!
Sound designer David Farmer looked high and low for the perfect sound for the baby Orcs in the 2001 movie *Lord of the Rings: The Fellowship of the Ring*. He found just what he was looking for when he heard a baby elephant seal. If you get a chance to see that classic movie, listen for the baby Orcs. Their sounds in the movie apparently didn't go through any special effects—they're all pure baby elephant seal!

Baby elephant seals are entirely helpless and for the first few weeks don't do much besides eat. They have to grow fast! After just one month, their moms will leave them alone on the beach, and they'll have to fend for themselves.
HOTSHOTSWORLDWIDE/DREAMSTIME.COM

It's obvious that this bad boy is making a whole lot of noise. Elephant seal vocalizations measuring up to 126 decibels have been recorded. That's louder than rock concerts and airplanes on takeoff.
EDURIVERO/GETTY IMAGES

WHO IS THE LOUDEST IN THE LAND?

Northern elephant seals are really, really loud!

How loud?

Elephant seal vocalizations have been measured at 126 decibels. This is one of the loudest mammal sounds ever recorded. And they *need* to be really loud. Because of their special in-water **adaptations**, elephant seals don't hear a lot of things as well as we do, especially low sounds and faraway sounds. They are sensitive to vibrations in the ground, and they can hear a higher range of frequencies than we can. This means that in order to hear one another when they're on land, they have to be able to make a real racket. And they do!

Just to put those decibels into perspective, 126 is *super* loud. Every 10 decibels represents *10 times* more noise than the previous marker. A dishwasher can be 80 decibels. A gas-powered lawnmower might be 90 decibels. So pretty loud. Anything from 91 to 100 decibels is considered *very* loud, and 101 to 125 is considered extremely loud. Planes taking off, loud concerts and trains are mostly in this range. Sounds of 126 decibels are considered painfully loud.

SOUTHERN COUSINS

Elephant seals belong to a scientific grouping called *Mirounga*. This grouping, known as a genus, has two species—*Mirounga leonina*, which is the southern elephant seal, and *Mirounga angustirostris*, which is the northern.

While the two species look a lot alike, it's easy to tell them apart. For one thing, you'll never see them side by side. There is no overlap in their territories. Both southern and northern elephant seals breed on land, but the southern species spends its time in subantarctic and antarctic waters, while the northern lives in the coastal waters off the west coast of North America, as far south as Baja California and California and as far north as the Gulf of Alaska. The northern seals migrate mostly to the southern part of their range when it's time to come on land for mating. So if you're looking at a picture of an elephant seal and see a penguin in the picture, you know you're looking at a southern elephant seal!

If you *were* to see them side by side, you'd still have no trouble telling them apart. While the male northern

If you see both elephant seals and penguins in a picture, you know you're looking at southern elephant seals. Penguins are not found in the range of the northern elephant seal. This noisy bunch is hanging with gentoo penguin chicks at Hannah Point on Livingston Island, part of the South Shetland Islands in Antarctica. TASFOTO/DREAMSTIME.COM

Researchers think this seal was from the Channel Islands, making him a northern elephant seal. What is known for sure is that his name was Goliath. He is shown hanging here with a zoo staff member at the Vincennes Zoo, Paris, in 1936. Goliath was grand, though, wasn't he? Even though his nose and overall size indicate that he was immature at the time the photo was taken, he still looks pretty big!
ACME NEWSPICTURES/STATE LIBRARY VICTORIA

WHAT'S IN A NAME?

There are specific terms for elephant seals at different ages. Here's how it breaks down:

Birth to one month: Pup
1–12 months: Weaner
1–2 years: Yearling
2–3 years: Juvenile or subadult
Adult (male): *Bull*
Adult (female): Cow

elephant seal is super big, the male southern is even bigger. The male northern can weigh up to 5,000 pounds (2,268 kilograms), while the southern can weigh as much as 8,000 pounds (3,629 kilograms).

To show you a comparison, a compact car weighs about 3,000 pounds (1,360 kilograms). A large truck or SUV can weigh about 5,500 pounds (roughly 2,500 kilograms). So while a male northern elephant seal is about the size of a *big* pickup truck, the southern is much larger. The only land animal that weighs the same or even more than the elephant seal is the African elephant. Elephant seals even weigh more than some whales, though whales win overall in the I'm-bigger-than-you-are category.

The other big difference between the species is the size of the proboscis—it's bigger on the northern species. Other than those differences, the two species are very similar. They eat the same stuff, migrate in the same way and do the same kinds of things while they're on land. They just do it all in *very* different places, and they'll never be neighbors or hang out.

A LIFE AT SEA

Elephant seals spend a crazy amount of time in the ocean. The juveniles and females are in the water ten months a year. The adult and nearly adult males are at sea for eight or nine months of the year.

When they're swimming, elephant seals break the surface of the water and breathe for a few minutes, then dive to hunt and feed. They'll dive deep for periods of 20 minutes to over an hour. Then they'll come back up, breathe for two to four minutes and dive again. All day. Every day. When they get back to their home beaches, they are fat (from all that eating!), but they are also super tired. They pull themselves onto the beach and fall into exhausted sleep.

SPEED AND GRACE

Northern elephant seals are not graceful on land. They bump along on their bellies, and although they can sometimes scoot very quickly over the sand, their made-for-swimming flippers will always slow them down.

But in the ocean it's a whole different story. They swim at speeds of up to 7.5 miles (12 kilometers) per hour. Everything that makes them awkward on land gives them speed and grace in the water. They keep their back flippers together and move them from side to side, which zooms the animals through the water quickly.

When they're going all out, they keep their front flippers close to the body. This streamlining aids in speed. When the seals are not going at full zoom, those flippers are used to steer, like the *rudder* on a sailboat, helping them change direction and navigate.

Elephant seals are also watertight while they're underwater. Special muscles close their nostrils and ears to

PINNIPEDS HAVE FINS!

Northern elephant seals are in the order Carnivora, suborder Caniformia. There are as many as nine extant families within Caniformia (three of these are the **pinnipeds**).

Pinnipeds are all carnivorous marine mammals with fin-like limbs. The word *pinniped* comes from Latin and means "fin feet." Harbor seals, sea lions and walruses are all pinnipeds too. Like other mammals, including humans, pinnipeds breathe air, even though (unlike humans) they spend most of their time in the ocean.

Elephant seals are among the best divers ever! They dive deeper and stay down longer than almost any other mammal does.
THOMAS P. PESCHAK/NATIONAL GEOGRAPHIC IMAGE COLLECTION/ALAMY STOCK PHOTO

Seals close special muscles in their nostrils and ears to prevent water from entering their bodies while on those deep dives.
FRANS LANTING STUDIO/ALAMY STOCK PHOTO

A SOLITARY JOB

When you see elephant seals on the beach, they seem so social. It's difficult to believe that in all the time they spend in the ocean—as much as 80 percent of their time—they are alone.

While they migrate and dive for food, they do so without company and without interaction with other elephant seals or other species.

prevent water from entering. These are the same muscles that keep their nostrils sealed when the seals are sleeping. It's the reason they sometimes look dead when they're sleeping on land—there's no breathing going on that we can see.

DOCTOR JEKYLL AND MISTER DIVE

Elephant seals have adapted to dive deeper and stay underwater longer than any other seal. When they dive, their bodies go through a physical transformation. First the heart rate slows, from their land-based norm of around 100 beats per minute to around 40 beats per minute.

Like Transformers, their bodies are geared to react in certain ways in different situations. While they dive, their blood doesn't flow through their whole body the way it does when they are on land—it actually *stops* flowing into their flippers and to any other places not necessary to keep the animal alive. It flows only to the brain, heart, kidneys, liver and lungs. In elephant seals—as in humans—these five organs are called the *vital organs* and are necessary for a mammal to survive.

Because everything but the vital organs goes into emergency shutdown mode when the seals are diving, they use much less oxygen. This is why elephant seals are the champion divers that they are.

Before a dive they push out all their breath. Then, because their lungs are empty, when they go *way* down they can dive without getting decompression sickness (also known as *the bends*). Even though they exhaled all the air they could before launching themselves down, the pressure in the deep sea helps to completely deflate their lungs. The lungs are made for this deflation and spring back into their original form when the seal resurfaces.

Elephant seals can also get oxygen from their blood. They have two times as much blood volume and 50 percent more red blood cells than a similar-sized land animal. They also have *myoglobin*, an oxygen storage system, in their muscles. They are fully equipped for long submersions!

One study has found that elephant seals have high amounts of carbon monoxide in their blood—the equivalent of a person who smokes 40 cigarettes a day. Scientists think there may be a connection between the carbon monoxide and their ability to dive to such extreme depths.

I'M SO SLEEPY!

A research team from Hokkaido University in Japan put satellite transmitters and data loggers on half a dozen young northern elephant seals and gathered data that shows they sleep as they dive. They can quickly sink to 500 feet (152 meters), then sleep while they drift more slowly into deeper water.

The data also showed that as they drift, the seals often roll onto their backs, stop actively propelling themselves and just spiral downward for 10 or 12 minutes at a time. The researchers called this the *falling-leaf phase* of their dive. The part of the descent when the animals are sleeping takes place deeper in the ocean than where orcas and sharks normally swim. That means that when they're sleep-dropping, elephant seals don't have to watch out for the predators that might pose a threat to them.

A young northern elephant seal diving in shallow water off Guadalupe Island, Mexico.
PASCAL KOBEH/ALAMY STOCK PHOTO

A young elephant seal eyes the camera with apparent interest and curiosity at Año Nuevo State Park in California.
TRAVIS WISE/FLICKR.COM/CC BY 2.0

SIZE MATTERS

Elephant seals are *sexually dimorphic.* This means that the males and females of the species look noticeably different. In addition to having a proboscis, male elephant seals are larger than female seals. Like, a lot larger. A male can weigh up to 5,000 pounds (2,268 kilograms). The average female, at just 1,600 pounds (726 kilograms), is substantially smaller.

The term *sexually dimorphic* doesn't relate to just differences in size and reproductive systems, and it doesn't apply just to elephant seals. Many birds are sexually dimorphic. The male birds often have elaborate and brightly colored feathers, while the females have a more muted color scheme and plumage.

Humans are also sexually dimorphic. In general, adult human males are 15 to 20 percent larger than adult females.

Like many (though not all) birds, mallard ducks are sexually dimorphic. The males are larger than the females, but they have some distinctly different physical characteristics as well.
NIKOLAY TCHAOUCHEV/UNSPLASH.COM

MY, WHAT BIG EYES YOU HAVE!

The elephant seal's eyes are really big. How big?

Diana Barnhart says elephant seal eyes are the size of tennis balls. She's a retired Los Osos Middle School science teacher and a long-time Friends of the Elephant Seal docent. Diana knows her elephant seals!

"It often looks like they are crying, because tears run down their cheeks," says Barnhart. They're not really tears, though, because elephant seals don't have tear ducts (and they don't have cheeks either). The *tears* are actually oily secretions that moisturize and protect the eyes and clear them of sand.

Those big eyes serve a purpose. When the seals are diving down to where the high-protein *bioluminescent* fish live, they need big eyes to help catch the small amount of light available in such a dark place. To help with this hunting-in-the-dark business, elephant seals have more rods than cones in their eyes, which means they don't see as much color as we do but are better at detecting movement. They also have a *tapetum lucidum*, which is a special layer of tissue in the eye that reflects light back to the retina, allowing elephant seals to see way better than we do in the dark. A lot of animals have this—dogs, cats and raccoons, to name a few. Humans don't—which explains why we need flashlights at night to find our way around while our pets have no problem at all.

Another thing that dogs and cats and elephant seals have that humans don't is a third eyelid. Officially called a *nictitating membrane*, this is a thin sheet of skin that is rich in blood vessels and lies between the eye and the lower eyelid.

Barnhart points out that in elephant seals, the nictitating membrane goes from side to side, "sort of like windshield wipers. The third eyelid has a moisturizing function with an oily layer next to the eyeball which helps remove sand when it goes across the eye."

ELEPHANT SEALS HAVE GOOD HEARING!

Even though elephant seals don't have visible earflaps, they can hear very well! Each elephant seal has two tiny holes in its head, just beyond the eyes. Each hole is very small—you really have to look to see it. When the elephant seal is underwater, the muscles contract tightly around the ear holes, and no water at all can get in. Beyond the tiny ear holes, the auditory passage that leads to the eardrum is

A study showed that a small group of female northern elephant seals is responsible for a large number of successful births each year. Researchers are calling them the Supermoms! Of the 7,735 female northern elephant seals at the Año Nuevo rookery, 6 percent of the females gave birth to 10 or more pups during their lifetime. That accounts for more than half the total pup population. This may be because the older the mom, the bigger she is, and the resulting pups are bigger too, making them better able to withstand the dangers and challenges that await them once they get off the beach.

LINDA L. RICHARDS

super narrow, but the inner ear chamber is equipped with all the normal internal hearing organs.

The inner chamber is larger than in other seal species though. The part of the inner ear called the *cochlea* helps to amplify incoming sound. It also helps give elephant seals good directional hearing, which is the ability to focus on sounds coming from a specific location.

HOME SWEET HOME

The place on land where elephant seals gather to breed, give birth, molt (shed the outer layer of hair and skin) and rest is known as a rookery, or *colony*.

In this elephant seal community, the high-ranking male gets to mate with more females, becoming what is known as a *beachmaster*. He can be responsible for 40 to 50 females, sometimes more. This group of females is called a *harem*. The beachmaster protects the females and their pups from other animals, including other male elephant seals looking to mate.

Males are much larger than females.
LINDA L. RICHARDS

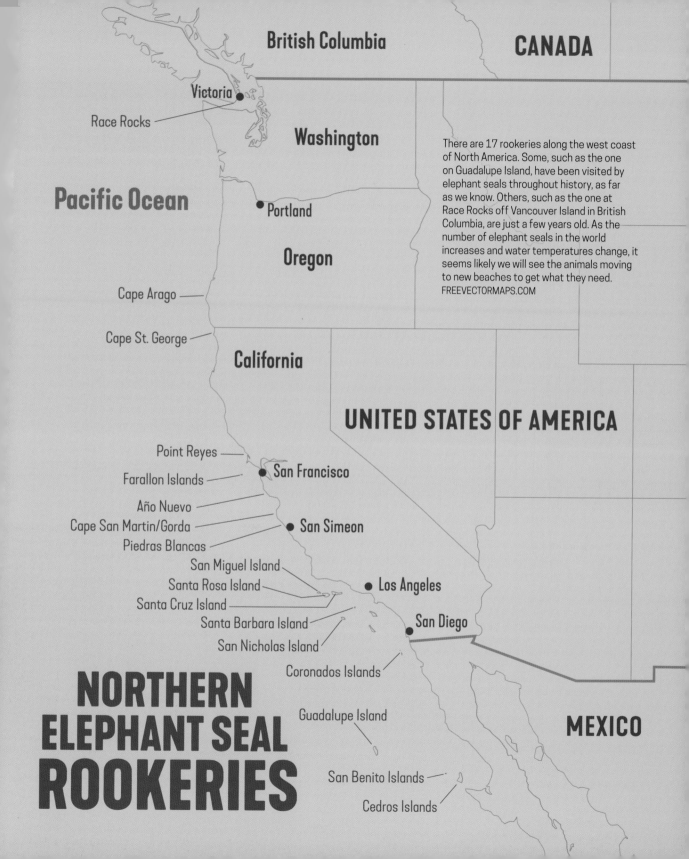

British Columbia

CANADA

Victoria

Race Rocks

Washington

Pacific Ocean

Portland

Oregon

There are 17 rookeries along the west coast of North America. Some, such as the one on Guadalupe Island, have been visited by elephant seals throughout history, as far as we know. Others, such as the one at Race Rocks off Vancouver Island in British Columbia, are just a few years old. As the number of elephant seals in the world increases and water temperatures change, it seems likely we will see the animals moving to new beaches to get what they need.
FREEVECTORMAPS.COM

Cape Arago

Cape St. George

California

UNITED STATES OF AMERICA

Point Reyes

Farallon Islands — San Francisco

Año Nuevo

Cape San Martin/Gorda — San Simeon

Piedras Blancas

San Miguel Island

Santa Rosa Island — Los Angeles

Santa Cruz Island

Santa Barbara Island — San Diego

San Nicholas Island

Coronados Islands

MEXICO

Guadalupe Island

NORTHERN ELEPHANT SEAL ROOKERIES

San Benito Islands

Cedros Islands

Not all bulls will earn the right to be a beachmaster. Only 10 percent of males each year get the chance to mate. The ones who aren't beachmasters sometimes lurk nearby, waiting for a chance to sneak in and mate, risking a fight with the dominant male. More often these non-dominant males hang out together, maybe to grumble about their fate in life. But the following year it will all begin again, and the previous year's losers, now older and stronger, will get another chance at having a harem of their own.

THE POLITICS OF THE ROOKERY

Achieving rank doesn't come without a fight. You see the males play fighting on the beach, even when they're babies. The fighting gets more serious as time goes on.

When the males enter puberty, each one begins to develop a *chest shield*. This thick skin consists of about 2 inches (5 centimeters) of cartilage over a 6-inch (15-centimeter) layer of *blubber*. The skin keeps getting thicker from the scarring caused by repeated fighting. This skin is often described as being *keratinized*, which means it's no longer alive but is now filled with a strong protein called keratin. Researchers aren't sure how the shield develops, but they *do* know that the older the animal, the

Young males face off, playing at the behavior that will later determine their place among their peers.
LINDA L. RICHARDS

This closeup shows the keratinized chest shield of the adult male.
SHEILA FITZGERALD/DREAMSTIME.COM

thicker and more pronounced the chest shield. On very mature males it looks almost painful, as though the skin is angry and broken. But it's not, and in more than one way it is keeping the elephant seal safe.

It's not often that anyone gets really hurt in the battles for dominance. And it's even more seldom that it is a fight to the death. A fight to the death would take a lot of effort, for one thing. And once on the beach, the seals won't be eating for a while. They need to conserve their energy!

In the first part of the fight, the males make a lot of noise. So *much* noise! Sometimes it alone is enough. Studies have shown that elephant seals remember skirmishes they've had in previous years. So when a male approaches another male and hears a big loud roar he recognizes, he might say to himself, "Hoooo boy. That's Jeff. Last year he really pushed me around. I'd better leave him alone." So he might back off peacefully and try his chances another day.

If the intruder decides to press his luck, the encounter will go from noise to a lot of pushing—chest shield to chest shield. Pushing and hollering. Remember, elephant seals can be *very* loud. Many fights stop right there. Between the hollering and the pushing, the two of them figure out who is stronger and, ultimately, more fit to sire a bunch of pups.

Only 20 percent of fights get beyond this pushing and hollering point, but when they do, it can be very scary. More pushing. More hollering. But now, at this higher level, there is also biting. Even these fights will rarely be to the death. More often one of the bulls will give up and back away, a move that is honored by the winning bull.

From the sidelines, fights between adult male elephant seals look super scary. These are large predators. When they're fighting, they're trying to sink their teeth into each other's chests. That's why their chest shields, with their deep network of scars, always look in danger of breaking open. But it's a dance, in a way, and only they seem to know all the rules.

This is a typical elephant seal family scene. While pups nurse, females and older youngsters soak up a bit of thin winter sun and flip sand endlessly. Meanwhile, the old beachmaster (left) and the young challenger (right) each state their position and identity. This encounter won't result in an altercation—the young male is not ready to be a beachmaster, if it's in his future at all. But maybe he'll be back for another challenge some other year.
LINDA L. RICHARDS

A YEAR IN THE LIFE OF AN ELEPHANT SEAL COLONY

There is never a time when an entire elephant seal population is on its home beach. Sometimes things are very quiet, and other times the beach is teeming with life.

January: This is a busy time on the beach. Pups are being born, there is some fighting for dominance among the adult males, and there is some breeding. By the end of the month, most of the new pups have been born.

February: Birthing and mating continue. The pups born the earliest start to be weaned as their moms leave for their migration.

March: The last few adults take their leave. The pups, now fasting, stay behind and learn the skills they'll need, through play in the safe, shallow waters just offshore.

April: The pups have all left on their first migration by late April, and the females and subadults return to the beach to start molting.

May: By the end of the month, the females and subadults are finished molting and are headed out on another migration.

June: Young males arrive back on the beach to molt.

July: Adult males arrive for their molt early in the month.

August: By mid-month, all molting is completed and the males have mostly left for their migration.

September: This year's pups return from their first migration.

October: Juvenile and subadult males begin to return from their migration, while far to the north, the females are diving deeply to fill up on squid.

November: As the month progresses, ever older males begin to arrive on the beach, returning from their migrations. By the end of the month mature males are arriving, and fights for dominance begin.

December: By the end of the month the males have all returned to the beach and are busy fighting for dominance. By then the females have also begun to return from their migration, and by the end of December, the first pups are being born.

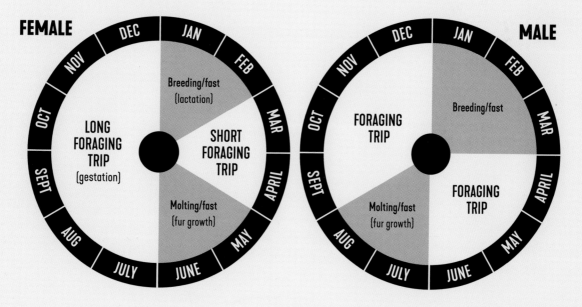

ADAPTED FROM FIGURE AFTER PETERSON ET AL 2016

Vn autre mõstre deſcrit par ledit Rondelet, en façon d'vn Eueſque, veſtu d'eſcaille, ayant ſa mitre & ſes ornements pontificaux, comme tu vois par ceſte figure, lequel a eſté veu en Polongne, mil cinq cens trente & vn, comme deſcrit Geſnerus.

Figure d'vn monſtre marin, ayant la teſte d'Ours, & les bras d'vn Singe.

Hieronymus Cardanus enuoya ce mõſtre icy à Geſnerus, lequel auoit la teſte ſem-blable à vn Ours, les bras & mains quaſi comme vn Singe, & le reſte d'vn poiſſon, & fut trouué en Macerie.

En la

2

THE ELEPHANT SEAL THROUGH THE AGES

THE ELEPHANT SEAL IN PREHISTORY

When you see a mature male northern elephant seal, it isn't hard to imagine you are looking, at least in part, at a prehistoric creature. In fact, it's been theorized that just this type of sighting had seventeenth century sailors claiming to have seen sea monsters.

It's also widely agreed that pinnipeds are the youngest group of marine mammals. They originated about 25 million years ago, during the late Oligocene period. By way of comparison, whales originated much earlier—more like 50 million years ago.

Northern elephant seals share a common ancestry with all other pinnipeds, but there is some debate about what that ancestry is, exactly.

Some scientists believe that pinnipeds are descended from bears. Others think they are descended from mustelids, which is the family that includes weasels, badgers, otters, wolverines and others. What makes this difficult to determine is that—evolutionarily speaking—

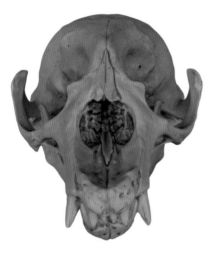

Compare the skull of the northern elephant seal (above) and the modern grizzly bear (below). Note the similarities and the differences. THE CALIFORNIA ACADEMY OF SCIENCES/SKETCHFAB.COM

pinnipeds split off from other caniforms 50 million years ago. Even though the evolutionary split was then, animals that resemble our modern-day pinnipeds didn't appear until later, at the end of the Oligocene *epoch* (some 29 million years ago).

Though the evolutionary trail is inconclusive, scientists agree that the elephant seal's most distant ancestors were land-based.

In the Oligocene epoch there was more open land, which meant animals could grow larger than they had during the Paleocene era some 30 million years before. It was during the Oligocene that early versions of many herd animals adapted to the plains as the rainforests from the previous epoch disappeared.

Even though elephant seals spend most of their time in the water, there are things about them that are more characteristic of a land animal than a sea creature. For example, their stomachs are simple and similar in structure to that of their land-bound relatives. And elephant seals are able to store extra oxygen in their blood for emergencies. Horses, and even humans in special circumstances, can do that too.

HOW DID THEY END UP LOOKING LIKE *THAT?*

Though elephant seals are not directly descended from bears, they share common ancestors. Both bears and elephant seals (and a whole lot of other species) are scientifically classified as being in the Animalia kingdom, the Chordata phylum, the class of Mammalia and the order of Carnivora. You and I are too! And so are a lot of creatures. But all seals are considered to be pinnipeds.

An artist's depiction of mammals of the Oligocene epoch. Note how they all look quite familiar yet also very different from the animals we know. That's because these are the ancestors of many of the mammals we know and love today. B. CHRISTOPHER/ALAMY STOCK PHOTO

WHAT'S THE OLIGOCENE?

Prehistoric times are broken into geologic epochs. In those periods temperature and other influences led to great changes on Earth and to the animals that lived here at the time.

The Oligocene epoch was part of the Cenozoic era, about 33.9 million to 23 million years ago. We can tell when it was by the way changes in the environment affected rock formations of that period.

During the Oligocene the tropical rainforests that had marked the Eocene (previous epoch) receded, giving way to broad grasslands and less tropical ecosystems. It was during the Oligocene that the first elephants with trunks, the earliest horses and the ancestor of the elephant seal and all pinnipeds, *Enaliarctos*, appeared on Earth.

Potamotherium might have looked like this. They and the more recently discovered *Puijila* could be part of the evolutionary trail that led to the elephant seal.
SMOKEYBJB/WIKIMEDIA.ORG

From there, though, there's not much agreement on anything other than the fact that pinnipeds are aquatic carnivores. With fins for feet!

ENALIARCTOS

The common ancestor that all pinnipeds seem to share is *Enaliarctos*. It lived from the late Oligocene epoch into the Miocene and evolved as a fish predator off the coast of western North America.

Enaliarctos's rear legs ended in flippers. It was a strong swimmer but could also use its back legs to get around on land. Skeletal evidence suggests that *Enaliarctos* used both foreflippers and hindflippers in swimming. Modern pinnipeds use one or the other. There is also skeletal evidence that *Enaliarctos* likely spent most of its time on land.

HUNTED TO EXTINCTION

Animals have been hunted for their fur and flesh for as long as people have been able to use tools. Seals were important to Indigenous people in the region since humans first began to inhabit the southwestern coast of North America 15,000 years ago.

The flesh of the elephant seal was an ideal subsistence food. The pelts of the animals, meant to keep the creatures cold at extremely low temperatures and in icy depths, could also help humans survive. And teeth and bones could be used as tools, *talismans* and musical instruments. As they did with the other creatures they hunted, the Indigenous people took only what they needed and used every part of the seal that they could.

Though Indigenous people traditionally hunted elephant seals, the number of seals they killed every year was so small it did not affect the population negatively. Once commercial elephant seal hunting in North America began in 1846, however, the picture changed quickly. The records of early hunters describe huge numbers and easy pickings. The animals would be shot or herded to one part of a beach and clubbed—females, males, young and old—and no one cared about anything but the oil in the animals' blubber. No other part of the animal was used. The blubber was taken, the oil was extracted from it, and the rest of the carcass was left to rot.

Before commercial elephant seal hunting, not a lot was known about the seals and their habits. No one really knew about their migrations or even where they spent their time. It wasn't until 1866 that northern elephant seals and their larger southern cousins were understood to be two distinct species.

Although it's hard to tell from the photo, this try pot is *big*. How big? Two adult men could sit inside it comfortably. It was used for rending the oil from the flesh of the various aquatic animals hunted over the years. A fire was lit under the pot, and the animals were cut up and put in the pot.
SMITH ARCHIVE/ALAMY STOCK PHOTO

WHAT'S A TRY POT?

The squeamish should look away. For the rest of you there's this…

A ***try pot*** was a specially designed vessel made to help rend the oil from whales, pinnipeds and penguins.

Try pots were mostly made from cast iron and had two flat sides. They were often built right into boats, in which case the whole structure—the pot and the wood that held it in place—was called the tryworks. Many sources credit the success of the American whaling industry to this ability to extract the oil from the blubber right at sea.

Once a whale, seal or penguin had been killed, blubber would be stripped from the carcass. Then the raw blubber would be cut into pieces and boiled in the try pots to extract the oil.

Pictured are southern elephant seals at an abandoned whaling station on South Georgia Island, a British territory in the southern Atlantic Ocean. Like their northern cousins, southern elephant seals were once hunted nearly to extinction, though their escape was not quite as narrow as that of the northern elephant seals. LIVERBIRD/DREAMSTIME.COM

OIL FOR LIGHT (AND OTHER IMPORTANT USES)

Whales—because of their size—were the creatures originally targeted as a source of oil. A single right whale would produce over 1,300 gallons (4,921 liters), and a single sperm whale over 500 gallons (1,892 liters) of oil from its head alone. But at the beginning of the California Gold Rush, whale populations off the west coast of North America had already been greatly reduced by hunting. And with large numbers of people entering the region as part of the migration west and the gold rush, there was an even greater demand for oil for lighting and manufacturing. Hunters turned their attention from the declining whale stock toward the abundant and placid elephant seal.

A large male northern elephant seal could provide over 200 gallons (757 liters) of oil. While this wasn't as much as a whale offered, elephant seals were easier to kill, as they spent a few months of every year out of the water.

By 1860 these were the prices for whale oil and the available alternatives:

Whale oil: $1.30 to $2.50 per gallon

Camphine: 50 cents per gallon

Lard oil: 90 cents per gallon

Coal oil (the original "kerosene"): 50 cents per gallon

Kerosene from petroleum: 60 cents per gallon

While there were various types of oil available to light homes and help machines run smoothly, they all had drawbacks. Lard oil, made from beef or pork fat, was considered low quality and kind of smelly when it burned. The same was true of coal oil, *and* it produced soot when it burned. Camphine—usually a mixture of turpentine and quicklime—was crude and unreliable. It created a bright light but could be smoky and smelly. Whale oil, and later seal oil, also burned on the smellier end of things, and both were expensive to produce. Not only did you have to send out boatloads of men to kill the whales or seals, but you had to do some work to get the oil after the animal was killed.

When kerosene made from petroleum was introduced after its discovery in 1846, it was considered a wonder oil. It burned more cleanly and was cheaper than other types of oil, in part due to government ***subsidies*** that helped get it accepted quickly. The subsidies worked. Today most countries depend on petroleum. There are good and bad things about that, but for the elephant seal, it was entirely good.

By the late 1800s, electric light was becoming available in many cities in North America. The need for oil to light homes and streets began to decrease, and by 1882 people thought there were no more elephant seals to hunt anyway.

The seals didn't know what hit them. They were easy targets and didn't even fight back.
VINCEVOIGT/GETTY IMAGES

But in order to find and kill seals, people had to learn as much as possible about the animals and their habits and, with all that valuable oil at stake, they didn't lose any time learning. Once people knew where and when the seals hauled out, they were easy pickings and hunters slaughtered them on the beaches.

Scientists don't know where the elephant seal population spent its time on land prior to 1840, but by the time commercial hunting of them had begun, the seals' rookeries were located on small islands near the coasts of northern Mexico and California. There are records from 1840 and 1846 showing northern elephant seals killed by sealers at Islas Los Coronados and at Santa Barbara Island in May 1840, and at Cedros and Guadalupe Islands in 1846.

C.M. Scammon del.

SEA-ELEPHANT. (MACRORHINUS ANGUSTIROSTRIS.) GILL.
1 MALE. 2 FEMALE.

A British naturalist and whaler named Charles Scammon saw northern elephant seals on his exploratory visit to the Pacific coast early in the 1800s. Scammon recorded everything he learned about the animals in a book called *The Marine Mammals of the Northwestern Coast of North America,* published in 1874, but he didn't write in his book that the animals he was sharing information about were being slaughtered to the point of extinction.

In 1852 Scammon was part of a sealing expedition in California. In five months, he reported being disappointed that he had collected only 350 barrels of oil, which was likely produced from 100 to 200 adult elephant seals. By the late 1870s, the species was considered extinct. But then in 1880 another small herd was discovered on the Baja California mainland. Over the next four years, all 335 of those seals were killed. Again, reports said the species was now truly extinct. Then three years later, 80 elephant seals were found and killed at Guadalupe Island off the Baja Peninsula. The following year another 4 were killed in the same spot. And now, the species was considered truly and finally extinct—except it wasn't.

From the look of this illustration, Charles Scammon was about as effective a conservationist as he was an artist. These "sea elephants" in his *Marine Mammals of the Northwestern Coast of North America* look pretty weird! FROM *MARINE MAMMALS OF THE NORTHWESTERN COAST OF NORTH AMERICA* BY CHARLES SCAMMON, PUBLISHED 1874.

Charles Haskins Townsend was director of the New York Aquarium at Battery Park from 1902 to 1937. The image shown here is from an album of photos he took on Guadalupe Island in March 1911 during an expedition on the USS *Albatross*. "Old male," he wrote in the album under this image. "Proboscis drawn up. Neck sore from fighting." CHARLES HASKINS TOWNSEND/WILDLIFE CONSERVATION SOCIETY ARCHIVES

SCIENCE AND PROTECTION

In 1892 naturalists Charles Haskins Townsend and Alfred Webster Anthony discovered nine northern elephant seals at Guadalupe Island. In the name of science, the men killed seven of the nine for the Smithsonian Institution. They considered the action "justifiable at the time" because, as Anthony explained later, "the species was considered doomed to extinction by way of the sealer's try pot and few if any specimens were to be found in the museums of North America."

Right up to and through 1911, elephant seals trickled into Guadalupe Island. Museum collectors for the Smithsonian killed them—4 in 1904, and 14 of 40 in 1907. (In 1930 American naturalist H.B. Huey would write that these killings had been "a severe stroke dealt to a struggling species, but the appetite of science must be satisfied.") Townsend went back to Guadalupe Island in 1911, killing 10 more seals. This time he left 125 alive, but he wasn't hopeful for the species—on the trip out, he'd looked for other individuals elsewhere and couldn't find any.

In 1922 a Mexican-American expedition was sent to Guadalupe Island to see if there were enough northern elephant seals remaining for the species to be preserved. Naturalists were surprised to find a thriving population of 262. The Mexican government decided to take strong steps to preserve them.

In what must have felt like a desperate and possibly pointless attempt to save the doomed species, the Mexican government banned the hunting of northern elephant seals and made Guadalupe Island a biological reserve. This gave the seals protection, as did the battalion that was left for a while on the island to protect them. A crude sign warned

Elephant seals don't actually smile. But sometimes, such as with this young pup, that's difficult to believe. It's even more difficult not to smile back.
LINDA L. RICHARDS

THE SMITHSONIAN INSTITUTION

The Smithsonian gets a hard time when the story of the northern elephant seal is told. However, the organization is a terrific and important one that has done much to save many species in its 170-years-plus history. It is the world's largest research and museum complex, comprising 19 museums and galleries, the National Zoological Park and numerous research centers. Since the days of the elephant seal–killing expeditions, much about the way we deal with nearly extinct species has changed. The scientists involved in those horrid events probably thought they were doing the world a favor, saving the image of the northern elephant seal for future generations when, in fact, they were bringing the fate of the entire species even closer to what seemed like an inevitable doom.

potential poachers, *Prohibit by law kill or capture elephant sea* [*sic*].

After the Mexican government decreed that the northern elephant seal was a protected species, the United States followed suit within a few years, as did Canada.

CHAMPIONS OF ADAPTATION

Once the Mexican government had stationed a battalion on Guadalupe Island to keep an eye on the seals and make sure no one was killing them, their numbers began to increase. Over the next few decades, elephant seals started to reclaim their historical territory, moving northward into the Channel Islands and beyond. They were first seen at San Miguel Island in 1925, and by the 1940s they had established a breeding colony there, hauling out at Point Bennett. By 1957 their population had risen to 13,000 animals.

I have this mental image of these poor survivor elephant seals on Guadalupe Island in 1922. They would have been blissfully unaware of it, of course, being seals with important seal things on their minds. But their escape had been so narrow! Wave upon wave of attackers, systematically taking them out. And now a few lucky ones, on the beach, catching their breath and dreaming about...well, probably nothing more than squid and bioluminescent protein snacks, but you get the idea.

They didn't waste any time. Well, why would they? There were babies to be born. There was fur and skin to molt. There were perilous journeys to navigate and deep dives to be made. Warm beaches to rest upon. There was just so much to do!

And that's what they did. Every year their numbers increased, until by 2020—not quite 100 years after the

A young elephant seal at molting time.
LINDA L. RICHARDS

The California state flag shows a California grizzly bear. The bears once hunted and ate baby elephant seals but have been extinct since 1924.

CALIFORNIA REPUBLIC

GRIZZLY BEARS IN CALIFORNIA

The California grizzly bear (*Ursus arctos californicus*), featured proudly on the state of California's official flag, has been extinct since 1922. Coincidentally, that is the year that the government of Mexico first protected the northern elephant seal.

The bears, once especially abundant along the California coast, were identified as public enemy number one by the cattle ranchers who first grazed their animals there. The ranchers weren't fond of the bears eating their cows and sheep, and they began a war on the bears that raged until the last one was shot and killed (or run out of state, depending on which version of the story you believe) in 1922.

California has been trying to reintroduce grizzly bears since 2014, but petitions to bring them back have been rejected every time people start talking about it. There's room to hope, though, especially since the California grizzly is supposed to be a good candidate for de-extinction or resurrection biology, which is a process that uses technology and existing species to recreate an extinct species.

It is beautiful at Piedras Blancas. But there are sharks waiting just beyond those rocks. Some of the baby seals won't make it out of the bay alive. Many rookeries are sited in this way, with beaches and protected rocky areas for babies to learn their lessons in safety. Elephant seals know what they're looking for in a new home.

Mexican government first proclaiming them protected—there were nearly a quarter million northern elephant seals, each year navigating the waters between their breeding grounds in Mexico and California and their distant hunting grounds in northern British Columbia and the Aleutian Islands. And it seems likely that the number will continue to grow.

HAPPY ENDINGS

It's been said that sometimes all that is needed for a species to recover is for people to stop killing them. This isn't always true, of course. Sometimes it's much more complicated than that. But certainly in the case of the elephant seal, not killing them was a big part of their recovery.

By the early 1900s, without oil hunters tracking them down and killing them, the northern elephant seal population had started to recover. The Pacific coast was bustling with young cities with growing populations. Because of that, many of the seals' traditional land predators, like bears and big cats, were gone, or were in low enough numbers to present no real threat to the by now increasing elephant seal population.

Left on their own with protection and no interference, the seals didn't just survive—they thrived. There has been a steady 6 percent increase in the population of northern elephant seals every year since 1922.

An elephant seal infant in the afternoon sun. LINDA L. RICHARDS

MODERN BREEDING GROUNDS

Today the home beaches of the northern elephant seal are in different locations than when the oil searchers first found the seals in the 1840s. This is in part because some of the rookeries now located on the mainland rather than

Where are they off to? These youngsters at Año Nuevo are far from the beach and look like they are on a mission of their own.
LINDA L. RICHARDS

islands had never been occupied by elephant seals (in the time that people have been recording such things). But it was also in part because, once the populations began to recover, after several years there was no longer room for all of the seals to shelter at their island homes. They needed to spread out!

Though there are still rookeries at Guadalupe, San Benito and Cedros Islands, and the Channel Islands near Santa Barbara in California, some of the very densest populations of elephant seals are in locations that would not have been their natural homes in the 1800s.

At Piedras Blancas, March and April are the busiest months of the year on the beach. The amount of elephant seal activity is astonishing. What's even more astonishing is that prior to 1990, there were no elephant seals at this location at all. The first elephant seal pup was born on the beach here in 1992—a surprise to the local residents, who were soon enchanted by this unusual occurrence. The number of births rose annually, and today Piedras Blancas is one of the busiest northern elephant seal rookeries.

So what happened?

While elephant seals may well have used these mainland spots in prehistory—and there is some archeological evidence to support this—by the time the nineteenth century rolled around, there were a lot of reasons for them to avoid mainland spots.

The biggest reason elephant seals avoided the mainland *prior* to the nineteenth century was predators.

Scientists have guessed that in the 15,000 years before whalers set their sights on the seals, the animals had at some point pulled up stakes and taken their business elsewhere. They abandoned the mainland rookeries they might previously have used and set up shop on mostly small islands in California and in Baja California, Mexico, where there were fewer land predators to threaten them.

There are still elephant seals that return each year to San Benito and Guadalupe Islands—places that were known as busy rookeries prior to the start of commercial sealing in the 1800s—but the most popular of the modern rookeries weren't inhabited by elephant seals at all until recently.

Nothing looks quite like an adult male elephant seal! But the babies are sure cute, and the females have that sweet face we tend to think of when we think of seals.
LINDA L. RICHARDS

Elephant seals are noisy communicators!
LEXI GOFORTH/GETTY IMAGES

3
THE CYCLE OF LIFE

A YEAR IN THE LIFE OF AN ELEPHANT SEAL

In December and January females return to their home beaches and begin giving birth. When the pups are born, they have black coats. When they are weaned a month later, they shed this fuzzy baby coat. Underneath will be a sleek silver coat, which will turn a brownish silver over the next year.

The mom elephant seal will stay with her baby for the first month of its life, looking after and nourishing the pup with her rich milk. She will stay until she is so hungry that she must return to the sea to begin the first of her two annual migrations, during which she hunts for food.

The average female will have lost roughly a third of her weight by the time she is ready to wean her pup. And while the mom is getting skinnier and skinnier, the baby is gaining about 10 pounds (4.5 kilograms) a day!

(ALMOST)
THE RICHEST MILK OF ALL

Humans make lots of decisions about milk. Should we have nut milk, like almond or cashew? If it's cow's milk, should it be whole milk (3.25 percent fat) or 2 percent?

When you consider that a baby northern elephant seal has to grow so much and so fast, it's no surprise that the milk those pups are fed has one of the highest fat contents of any animal's. In fact, people who have seen elephant seal milk compare it to a milky pudding.

PERCENTAGE OF FAT IN MILK
Elephant seal: 50
Cat: 11
Human: 5
Cow: 3.25
Black rhino: 0.02

The pups weigh 70 to 90 pounds (32 to 41 kilograms) when they are born. When they are weaned, they are called *weaners*. At that time, they will weigh on average from 250 to 300 pounds (113 to 136 kilograms) but can weigh up to 600 pounds (272 kilograms), at which point they are known as superweaners!

Mating occurs about three weeks after the female gives birth. Elephant seals are capable of what is called *delayed implantation*. Once conceived, the fertilized egg doesn't implant and begin development until conditions are right. It stays inside the mother in a dormant state until seven and a half months before the pup is born, which occurs in mid- to late January.

After the pups are weaned, the mothers leave, embarking on their migration. They will cover about 11,000 miles (17,700 kilometers). The males' migration is longer—13,000 miles (20,920 kilometers)—but the females go farther out and dive deeper than the males do.

Although scientists don't know for sure why the journeys of each gender are so different, they think that females encounter fewer predators farther out to sea and also need to get the richest supply of food available to nourish the pup that is growing inside them.

The sharks and orcas that prey on elephant seals are more likely to do so in the shallow coastal waters, which male elephant seals traverse on their migrations. But because the males are so much bigger than the females, those predators are less of a threat to the males.

Nothing about these migrations is accidental, as researchers have observed the same animals turning up on the same beaches year after year. The elephant seals know just where they're going!

Once March rolls around, pretty much all the adults have left the rookeries, and the new pups are on their own. They'll have had about 28 days with their mothers and will have spent most of that time eating. Now that they're on their own, the pups have to quickly learn how to swim and dive, because with Mom gone, they can't eat again until they start their own migrations.

During this period it's possible to see the youngsters out in the water together, spending time doing what looks like playing. But it's actually

PUT THAT BABY ON HOLD!

Elephant seals aren't the only species that can use delayed implantation, also called *embryonic diapause*, as a strategy for survival. Even though embryonic diapause has been observed in only 2 percent of all species, scientists theorize that all mammals, including humans, may have had this ability but lost it as they evolved because the strategy was no longer needed.

But for animals such as roe deer, armadillos, kangaroos and other marsupials, bears, bats, badgers and all pinnipeds, including elephant seals, things are more uncertain. In the case of elephants seals, delayed implantation means that the baby doesn't start to grow until food is abundant and the mother's instincts tell her that she can expect safe conditions at the end of the pregnancy, which for northern elephant seals is a period of about 291 days—roughly seven and a half months. Until it implants in the uterus, the fertilized egg stays dormant. And that's how it happens that all those baby elephant seals are born within a few weeks of each other every January, even if the moms got pregnant months apart.

By the time they are weaned, the babies are fat! They need to be—they won't get a meal for a few months, while they learn the swimming and hunting skills needed for their first migration.
LINDA L. RICHARDS

On their migrations elephant seals are totally alone, out of contact with others of their kind. In the rookeries, though, elephant seals seem openly affectionate with each other, frequently cuddling together, sometimes playing and communicating.
LINDA L. RICHARDS

THE LONG-HAUL TRUCKERS OF THE SEA!

No other mammal's migration is as long, both in time and distance traveled, as an elephant seal's. As a result, the seals are really depleted when they get back to their home beaches. That's when they're ready to haul out.

The term *haul-out* is borrowed from the maritime world. It refers to the time, usually once a year, when a boat moored on the water is hauled out to fix it up and make it seaworthy again. It's the time to scrape off barnacles and fill any holes or cracks. Elephant seals don't have barnacles growing on them, and they don't develop any holes or cracks, but they do need their time off, which is spent on the beach.

part of learning the skills they need to navigate dangerous waters on their own.

At Piedras Blancas, the docents call this Weaner School, and if you watch the seal pups from the shore, it really does look like they're out there teaching each other to swim.

In late April and early May, the adult females return to their home beaches to start their annual molt. The males, who have traveled farther to find their food, start to arrive in June and deeper into summer.

After the molt, everyone heads back into the water, so late summer is when there is the least amount of activity to see on the beaches, as the seals are at sea.

In November the junior males begin their *haul-out*. The mature males start to arrive on the beach in November and December, glossy and well fed from a season of eating in northern waters. They continue to arrive until December and January, when the females arrive and begin giving birth.

And then the cycle starts all over again.

A CATASTROPHIC MOLT

Molting is the periodic shedding of hair, skin, feathers, nails, shells, horns…anything that is lost regularly but can grow back. Even humans molt! Humans shed their entire outer layer of skin almost every month. That means you're losing as much as 0.003 ounces (0.085 grams) of skin flakes every hour. Ewwwwwwwww!

We also molt the hairs on our head. The average person has about 100,000 hairs on their head and loses as many as 150 *every day*. We humans are in constant renewal.

Elephant seals are *not* in constant renewal. They go through what is called a **catastrophic molt**. That means, essentially, that everything comes off over the course of a few weeks rather than bit by bit over time. Every last hair on the body *and* the skin it is attached to—off!

Though a number of species have a catastrophic molt—snakes, crabs, a bunch of reptiles and insects—only a couple of semi-aquatic animals do. One is the elephant seal, and the other is the penguin, whose downy baby feathers, meant for insulation on land, need to be transformed into the sleek skin that will protect them in subzero water and help them skim effortlessly through the sea.

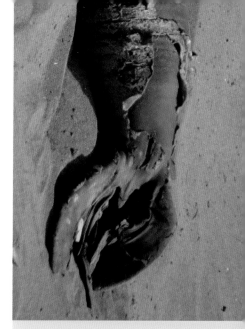

The orange tag on this seal shows that it was rescued and has now been released back into the wild (see page 67 to see what each color tag indicates).
LINDA L. RICHARDS

Elephant seals are one of the few species that have a catastrophic molt each year. Their hair and skin come off in long strips. It looks like they are falling apart!
LINDA L. RICHARDS

Northern elephant seals have fins! Elephant seals have underdeveloped hind limbs whose ends form the tail and tail fin. Each "non-foot" ends in five long, webbed fingers, which the seals use to help them swim, to protect themselves from other predators and for scratching an itch.
LINDA L. RICHARDS

SHINY AND NEW

All that time an elephant seal spends underwater, with blood flow to the skin restricted, has a price. The skin dies, so every year a whole new suit of skin and hair is created underneath the old one. All that old skin and hair is sloughed off, and a shiny new animal emerges. While the seal rests on the beach, blood is able to reach the skin without interruption or big changes in temperature.

A study from the University of California, Santa Cruz showed that at least part of the reason elephant seals shed their skin annually is to rid themselves of toxins such as mercury, which never disappears or evaporates on its own. Because they are a *top-level predator*, elephant seals eat a diet high in mercury. The mercury concentration in their bodies may be 1 to 10 million times *higher* than the mercury levels of the seawater.

Molting is not something elephant seals can do in the water. They are able to dive deeper and into colder waters than any other mammal can because their bodies have evolved in such a way that when they are diving, their blood is busy keeping their internal organs warm and protected. For the skin and hair to come off, however, the

WHY ALL THE SAND FLIPPING?

If you spend time watching elephant seals on land, you will see them flipping sand around. Researchers think there are many reasons why they might do this.

The seals may do it to cool off when they are on land. Also, the sand can act as a natural sunscreen. They will sometimes flip sand protectively, such as when a male's approach is unwanted. New moms will also flip sand over the **afterbirth**, which is what is left of the organ that grows to protect and feed young mammals in the womb. Moms also flip sand over new pups who have died. Elephant seals have even been observed flipping sand when they're under stress.

While watching them flip the sand, you will also see the seals being amazingly flexible in scratching themselves with their five-fingered foreflippers. You can even see tiny pups scratching themselves—perhaps because of bugs, molting skin or just general itchiness!

Elephant seals flip sand to cool themselves off, to provide a sunscreen and sometimes even to protect themselves. Elephant seals flip sand a lot!
LINDA L. RICHARDS

blood has to be at the surface of the skin. Catastrophic molting increases blood flow to the surface of the skin to supply nutrients to the new skin and fur underneath.

Not only does this mean that the seals have to be on land so their blood isn't busy elsewhere, but scientists have noted that the animals are more susceptible to temperature changes when the molt is in progress and they're down to their new suits. Though they don't eat or swim very far during the time the molt is in progress, they'll often move to the water's edge where it's cooler.

The whole molting process takes a few weeks, and the seals look pretty funny while it's happening. The old skin comes off in strips and chunks. It just sloughs off on its own, without much discomfort to the animal. It might cause some itchiness, but not pain.

Watching a seal molt isn't the most exciting viewing. It's interesting though. And there's something so promising about seeing that sleek new pelt underneath the hair and skin being shed and a new golden creature emerging from underneath!

Elephant seals spend most of their time awake and on the move. But when they are on land, they mostly rest.
LINDA L. RICHARDS

HOW DOES MERCURY GET INSIDE A FISH?

Mercury is a chemical element that is toxic to the central and peripheral nervous systems. If you breathe in mercury, it can be dangerous, even deadly. It also **bioaccumulates**. That means your body (or the body of a fish or a seal) doesn't just get rid of it like it does many other toxins. Instead, mercury builds up inside you until you either get really sick or do something on purpose to get rid of it.

We know mercury isn't good, so how does it get inside fish?

One of the ways is through pollution that enters the lakes and oceans, contaminating the food eaten by the fish. However, some scientists think that there may also be some natural mercury inside fish or that they get it from sources other than or in addition to pollution. This is because as mercury levels in the atmosphere have gone up, the levels of mercury inside fish have stayed the same.

We do know that each time a fish contaminated with mercury gets eaten, the mercury becomes more concentrated. Imagine some algae that contains small amounts of mercury. A tiny fish eats the algae and gets more mercury inside it than the algae does. Then the tiny fish gets eaten by a small fish, which means even *more* mercury. The small fish gets eaten by a bigger fish, and so on.

So fast forward to the elephant seal. They are high-level predators. By the time *they're* eating a fish (or crab or octopus or squid or...), their food has been on that predation chain for quite a while! The seals end up *full* of mercury. And how to get rid of it? You guessed it—the catastrophic molt.

NORTHERN ELEPHANT SEAL MIGRATION MAP

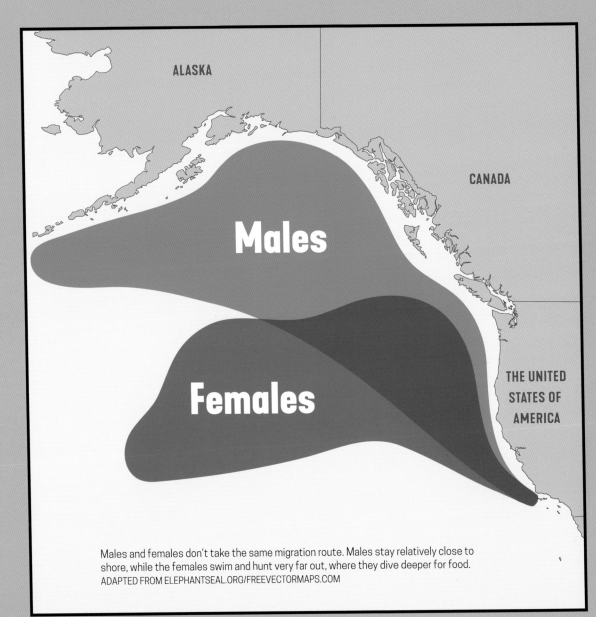

ALASKA

CANADA

Males

Females

THE UNITED STATES OF AMERICA

Males and females don't take the same migration route. Males stay relatively close to shore, while the females swim and hunt very far out, where they dive deeper for food.
ADAPTED FROM ELEPHANTSEAL.ORG/FREEVECTORMAPS.COM

HUNTING AND FORAGING

Being an elephant seal means months and months of swimming and hunting and working hard at getting fat.

The males hunt from Washington State to the western Aleutian Islands in Alaska. On their foraging trips, they stay within 12 miles (19 kilometers) of the *continental shelf*, where they eat hagfish, hake, small sharks, skates and rays.

Compared to the hunting that the females do, it's easy pickings for the males to get lots of protein-rich food. But it's also not safe. One in three male elephant seals don't make it back to the rookery, losing their lives to sharks and orcas on their dangerous journey.

The females hunt almost entirely in the open ocean off the Pacific coast of North America. They forage, on average, 335 miles (539 kilometers) from the continental shelf, where they dive deep in order to find lantern fish, octopus and different kinds of squid that are really rich in the proteins elephant seals need.

LINDA L. RICHARDS

While their dives are super difficult and they dive much, much deeper than the males, only one in seven female elephant seals won't make it home. Since a single male can be the father of many elephant seal pups each year, the survival of the female is more important to the future of the species than the survival of the male. It might be that the seals' different feeding patterns are nature's way of making sure more females survive their migrations.

Not only do the males and females not hunt together when they're in the ocean, but they also don't even hang out with their own gender. Instead they operate as self-directed hunting machines with laser-like focus. They need to get fat enough that by the time they return to their home beaches, they'll be able to go for many weeks without eating again.

WOULD AN ELEPHANT SEAL THINK I AM DELICIOUS?

Elephant seals are carnivores and the top-level or **apex predator** in their class, but they never, ever eat humans. In fact, a lot of what they eat is so teeny, it slips right down their throats whole. Slippery little squids and octopuses and things that are even smaller but high in nutrition and calories.

That said, it is possible that if you were in its territory, an elephant seal *might* hurt you, even if just by accident, for although they are super gentle, they are also very big.

And even though elephant seals are generally docile, there are exceptions. In 2007 there were reports of a large male elephant seal in the Russian River in California who was nicknamed Nibbles because he bit a surfer who fell on him.

In 2011 two professional divers and camera people shared footage of being attacked by an elephant seal. They were on assignment for *Animal Planet*. The footage shows them first cuddling with a huge adult male, then reacting in surprise when the animal seems to attack them. "My head was kind of resting on his tongue," the diver said at one point. "I was afraid for my life!" And well he should have been. It's important to always use caution when interacting with wild animals and to keep your distance from them. Even if they look sweet and cuddly, you don't know what their instincts might make them do.

Young elephant seals play-fighting in the shallow water just off the rookery at Año Nuevo State Park. As it does with other mammals, play helps prepare them for the work they'll do as adults.
ANCHOR LEE/UNSPLASH

COOKIECUTTER SHARKS

Though by their name it sounds like they might be cute, cookiecutter sharks are really not! Although they are pretty ugly and also dangerously irritating, these sharks are very small, so their attacks aren't lethal to elephant seals.

The largest male cookiecutter sharks are 17 inches (43 centimeters) long. The females are slightly larger at around 22 inches (56 centimeters). Since an average male northern elephant seal is about 13 feet (3.9 meters) long, an attack by this shark doesn't pose much of a threat. It would be like you or me being attacked by a kitten or a guinea pig. Cookiecutter sharks take cookie-sized bites out of their prey, and at a number of rookeries in warm waters, you can see elephant seals with cookie-sized scars on their bodies.

MEET THE FAMILY

There are 34 species of pinnipeds in the world today, including 16 species of eared seals and 18 species of true seals. In addition, walruses are also classified as pinnipeds. Here's a look at the pinniped families.

PHOCIDS (EARLESS SEALS OR TRUE SEALS)

These pinnipeds have ear holes but no external ear flaps. They also have small foreflippers. On land they kind of scoot along on their tummies. In the ocean, though, they really get going. They propel themselves through the water by moving their rear flippers forward and backward in the same way that a fish uses its tail. The elephant seal is classified as a phocid.

ODOBENIDS (WALRUSES)

Walruses are one of the largest pinnipeds. Males can weigh over 3,000 pounds (1,361 kilograms). Males and females both have tusks, and their mouths are designed for siphoning up shellfish from the ocean floor. They can inflate the air sacs in their necks, allowing them to float.

OTARIIDS (EARED SEALS)

Pinnipeds in the third family, Otariidae, are referred to as otariids or eared seals. As you'll have guessed, these guys have ears, or at least little external earlike flaps, where the true seals and the walruses do not. Their flippers are relatively large for the seals' body size. They swim using their front flippers like the oars of a boat and walk when they are on land. Sea lions and fur seals are both examples of otariids.

Cookiecutter sharks are ugly *and* nasty. They disguise themselves as normal little fish that a lot of creatures might like to eat. Then, when something gets close, they attack with their incredibly efficient teeth, tearing circular bites out of their prey. The shark bites are so small that they usually won't kill an elephant seal, but many seals have scars from attacks by these little guys. NATIONAL OCEANIC AND ATMOSPHERIC ADMINISTRATION

A curious harbor seal in Boothbay Harbor, ME.
KEITH LUKE/UNSPLASH.COM

The walrus is a pinniped further classified as an Odobenid. There used to be several other members of the Odobenidae family, but only two subspecies of walrus are left, the Pacific and the Atlantic. Both live in the cold waters near the Arctic Circle. Walruses are among the largest pinnipeds, with males weighing up to 4,400 pounds (about 2,000 kilograms). JAY RUZESKY/UNSPLASH.COM

Cape fur seals all have external ear flaps.
They also look kind of disapproving of the camera!
DAVIDE DALFOVO/UNSPLASH.COM

MAXIMUM DEPTH COMPARISON

THE INSIDE SCOOP

What do elephant seals and top performing athletes have in common? It turns out that both of them have developed the ability to store extra oxygen in their spleen.

All creatures with a backbone or spinal column (vertebrates) have a spleen. The spleen filters blood and helps fight infection. But in mammals that dive or exercise heavily, the spleen has an additional function. It can serve as a kind of oxygen tank to store blood. Blood stored in this way is very thick, sticky and full of red cells, which hold extra oxygen. This extra oxygen can be injected into the blood when it is needed. A horse or a human athlete will get this kind of oxygen injection while doing a heavy workout, but in diving mammals like the elephant seal, the process is taken to a different level. Even more oxygen is available to the animal—which is good, because being so deep underwater, the seal needs it!

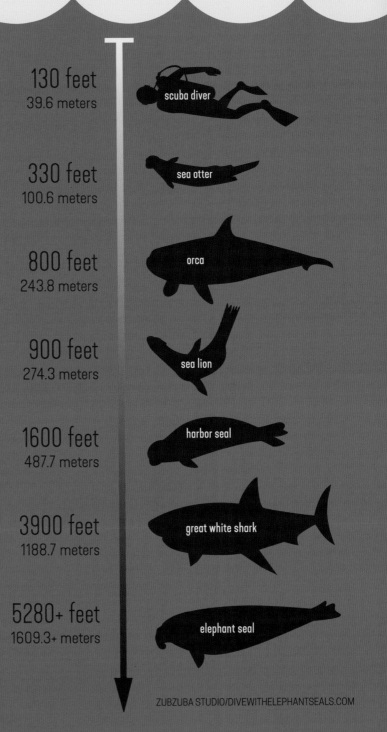

130 feet
39.6 meters
scuba diver

330 feet
100.6 meters
sea otter

800 feet
243.8 meters
orca

900 feet
274.3 meters
sea lion

1600 feet
487.7 meters
harbor seal

3900 feet
1188.7 meters
great white shark

5280+ feet
1609.3+ meters
elephant seal

ZUBZUBA STUDIO/DIVEWITHELEPHANTSEALS.COM

FASTING ON THE BEACH

With the exception of the newborn pups who are fed their mom's milk, elephant seals don't eat while they are on the beach. Ever.

The only water available to elephant seals when they are on land comes from burning the fat and protein in their tissue. This is called fat *oxidation* and, yes, that's right—their own bodies feed them.

The whole time they are on land, northern elephant seals get smaller and smaller as they lose body weight. This isn't a couple of pounds bigger or smaller after eating too much at Christmas either. Both genders lose about one third of their weight during their haul-outs.

If an average male weighs 4,000 pounds (1,814 kilograms) when he arrives, by the time he leaves to begin his next migration, he will weigh only 2,600 pounds (1,180 kilograms), having lost about 1,400 pounds (635 kilograms). A female elephant seal of 1,600 pounds (726 kilograms) will lose just over 500 pounds (227 kilograms)—about the weight of an average piano.

The fact that elephant seals don't eat when they're on land makes them pretty desirable house guests, aside from that fishy smell. But when they crawl back into the sea, they are tired, hungry and a lot smaller than when they arrived!

LINDA L. RICHARDS

NO BATHROOM BREAKS!

Elephant seals don't drink seawater. When they're in the ocean, they extract the moisture they require from their prey. When they're hauled out and spending months on the beach, they are not ingesting fresh water, and their bodies have gone into a special shutdown mode that enables them to conserve every bit of moisture and food energy they can. With nothing coming in, there is very, very little to come out. When they are in this super-conserving mode, their urine is ultra concentrated and filled with impurities the body needs to get rid of.

One study showed that the average elephant seal pup (a month after weaning) might pee 2.3 fluid ounces (68 milliliters) per day and that urine will contain mostly waste and not much water. By comparison, the average human pees about 27 to 67 fluid ounces (800 to 2,000 milliliters) per day—and we weigh much, much, much less than an elephant seal pup!

All of this is true for poo as well. It's the garbage in/garbage out principle—with nothing going in, nothing is coming out!

LINDA L. RICHARDS

WHAT AND WHO EATS *THEM?*

The adult male northern elephant seal is at the top of its food chain, so there is no land animal that would attack it in order to eat it. Great white sharks and orcas *do* prey on northern elephant seals, especially adult males on their migration and seal pups and juveniles.

The rookeries are sited with just this danger in mind. They are always on beaches that have a lot of shallow water near shore, as sharks need deep water to hunt. The shallow water means the pups can safely play their learning games—swimming, fighting and socializing—without being eaten by a shark.

As peaceful as the beach looks, there's a whole other world out there. At Piedras Blancas (shown), as at other rookeries, there are shallow waters close to shore suitable for playing, learning and bathing. But just beyond that craggy rock sharks lurk, waiting for the unlucky elephant seals that won't make it any farther. LINDA L. RICHARDS

A male emerges from the water at Drakes Beach, Point Reyes.
XAVIER HOENNER/GETTY IMAGES

4

THE ELEPHANT SEAL TODAY

GARBAGE IN THE OCEAN

Until big changes are made to international rules about who can use the ocean in what way, the threats to marine life will continue to mount. This is true not just for elephant seals, but for all of the creatures who live in the ocean. More people fishing mean more nets and lines for animals to get tangled in, more boats that might hit them and more debris floating in the sea.

The good news is that as the threats to the health of our oceans have increased, so has awareness of the problems and a search for solutions. Nonprofit organizations like the Ocean Cleanup and Ocean Voyages Institute are working hard to fix some of the environmental problems affecting elephant seals and other ocean dwellers.

KIDS SAVING THE WORLD

The Ocean Cleanup was developed by inventor and whiz kid Boyan Slat when he was just 18. Slat, who was born in 1994, dropped out of university to pursue his passion—ridding the ocean of plastic.

Slat was always inventing things. When he was 14, he set a Guinness World Record when he launched 213 water rockets—model rockets using water as part of their power source—at the same time.

When Slat was 16 he went on a fishing trip to Greece and was shocked when he encountered more plastic than fish. It made him realize he wanted to do something about it.

Slat founded the Ocean Cleanup in 2013. The organization raised US$2.2 million through crowd-funding and another $31.5 million through corporate partnerships and sponsorships. The funding has enabled the Ocean Cleanup to send out boats equipped with Slat's special ocean-cleaning technology. They have also announced a plan for a second phase that will intercept plastic that comes to the ocean by way of the 1,000 most polluting rivers in the world. According to the Ocean Cleanup, these 1,000 rivers are responsible for 80 percent of the plastic that ends up in the ocean each year.

This extended cork line is from the Ocean Cleanup's 001/B system. The buoys keep the net afloat while it scoops plastic out of the ocean. The system is designed to use the natural forces of the ocean to passively catch and concentrate plastic.
COURTESY OF THE OCEAN CLEANUP

The ultimate mission of the Ocean Cleanup is to remove 90 percent of floating plastic by the year 2040. In 2019 alone, the Ocean Voyages Institute scooped 40 tons (36 metric tonnes) of abandoned fishing nets—also known as *ghost nets*—out of the *Great Pacific Garbage Patch*.

WARMING WATERS

Garbage isn't the only environmental factor having an impact on elephant seals. Climate change is causing the temperature of the ocean to rise. There's a relatively small new rookery at Race Rocks off Vancouver Island in British Columbia. This might indicate that warming waters have some elephant seals looking for a cooler home beach. And not only are the waters in the north cooler, it's also less of a drive to get groceries!

Dr. Patrick Robinson is the director of Año Nuevo Reserve and a lecturer at University of California, Santa Cruz. He says seals are master migrators, and they will likely be able to adapt as their food sources move north. "We are seeing new colonies pop up in northern California and Oregon," he says. "But it's hard to know if this is climate-related or a result of population expansion."

So while elephant seals making their home on land farther north might have to do with climate change, it also might just be because—with their successful comeback—beaches to the south are getting pretty crowded!

SCIENCE AND THE SEAL

One thing about the future of the elephant seals we know for sure is that we will have a lot more knowledge about them available to us than we did in the past. That's because

Plastic in the ocean is a huge problem.
BRIAN YURASITS/UNSPLASH

One of Dr. Michael R. Wing's students participating in the Elephant Seal Monitoring Project. LINDA L. RICHARDS

ELEPHANT SEALS IN SCHOOLS

Between 2011 and 2015, students at Sir Francis Drake High School in San Anselmo, California, read tags and counted northern elephant seals at the Point Reyes National Seashore. The different color tags include a number that matches a particular elephant seal. For example, a red tag with the number 805 would relate to an animal tagged on a specific date on San Nicolas Island.

The Elephant Seal Monitoring Project was dreamed up and run by science teacher Dr. Michael Wing. Working with Dr. Sarah Allen, a senior National Park Service biologist, the students used spotting scopes to read the numbers on the colored tags relating to each elephant seal colony. They then added the data to the NPS database and analyzed it themselves.

The students were trying to answer two questions: Do young seals stay with members of their birth cohort even when they migrate to other, faraway beaches? And do young seals explore other beaches but return to the beach where they were born when it's time to reproduce?

Dr. Wing says having young people involved in both the collection and application of data was a great exercise for everyone. It let the kids know what it feels like to be on an important scientific mission, while adding hands to a job that can't have too many—the collection of data on the northern elephant seal.

dedicated and passionate researchers are collecting more and more data on them all the time.

There are researchers working at several colonies. Collectively they manage to place tags on the flippers of 1,000 to 2,000 animals each year. In addition to the animals that are flipper tagged, as many as 40 female elephant seals are tagged electronically and equipped with tracking devices each year. These electronic tags have given scientists a huge amount of data about the seals' lives, including depth of dives and annual migrations.

Dr. Daniel Costa is an ecologist and biologist at the University of California, Santa Cruz. He says the data collected via the electronic tags has contributed hugely to the understanding of the elephant seal's life at sea. Before electronic tags documented exactly where elephant seals were going on their migrations, researchers thought the animals all stayed pretty close to the coast. Previously researchers could survey seals only by ship or plane, which limited where they could look.

The electronic tags helped researchers learn how far offshore the females wandered and showed that individual animals took the same route, year after year.

Every year as many as 40 female elephant seals are fitted with a lightweight electronic tracking device. It is glued on using epoxy but is easily removed by researchers and does not hurt the animal in any way or hinder its migration. The data the signals from the devices bring back has altered researchers' understanding of elephant seal migration. PINNIPEDA AT THE ENGLISH WIKIPEDIA/CC BY-SA 3.0

"The other surprise," says Dr. Costa, "was how deep they dive and that they spend most of their time underwater. They were much better divers than any other marine mammal studied to date. The only group that exceeds them is beaked and sperm whales."

WHERE AND HOW TO SEE THEM

Sometimes I still find it hard to believe that not so long ago, experts thought all the northern elephant seals in the world were gone forever. Some 100 years later there are almost a quarter of a million of them, doing their twice-yearly migrations and swimming farther and diving deeper than most people can even imagine.

One of the bonuses of the boom in the northern elephant seal population is that if you want to see these special creatures with your own eyes, you can. You can get quite close to them at Año Nuevo near Santa Cruz, California. From December 15 to March 31 of every year, you can sign up to join a docent-led tour that gets you right on the beach with the seals. It's thrilling to be so close, as you really experience the noise (and the smell!) they make when they're on the beach. It's a 3- to 4-mile

Between December 15 and March 31, you can sign up for docent-led tours at Año Nuevo State Park, one of the places where elephant seals are studied most heavily due to the park's proximity to University of California, Santa Cruz.
LINDA L. RICHARDS

The boardwalk at Piedras Blancas. Note the seals on the beach and the parking lot in the background. And there are no bathrooms on-site.
LINDA L. RICHARDS

(4.8- to 6.4-kilometer) hike to get to where the seals are, some of it on boardwalks and some of it on sand dunes. On my last guided trip, our group came across a small band of juveniles in the dunes—not a typical place for them to be. They were curious but only mildly interested in us—possibly busy with whatever teenage expedition they were on!

The best place to really get a sense of northern elephant seals in their natural habitat is at Piedras Blancas near San Simeon, California.

The beach the seals have selected there is below some high-bank waterfront, and the splendid local organization that watches over them is called Friends of the Elephant Seal. The friends have constructed a 6-mile (9.7-kilometer)-long boardwalk along the cliffs, about 40 feet (12 meters) above the seals. The seals seem completely unbothered by the thousands of people that flock to see them annually. Here you can see the seals breeding and birthing, fighting and learning, and though you're not quite close enough most of the time to smell them, you can hear their loud voices very well!

Looking down at the rookery at Point Reyes National Seashore, near San Francisco. SNYFER/DREAMSTIME.COM

POINT REYES

There is a small colony of northern elephant seals at Point Reyes, about 30 miles (48 kilometers) north of San Francisco, although you won't see as many seals here as you will at other places, especially Piedras Blancas.

The traditional viewing spot at Point Reyes has been an area protected by the US National Park Service. From Point Reyes National Seashore park you can access a couple of overlooks high above the cliffs where elephant seal behavior is best viewed with binoculars. However, during the US government shutdown in 2019, elephant seals made international news by taking over a public beach in the park. Docents were on hand to help visitors understand what they were seeing and to instruct them about keeping a safe distance. That shutdown has had far-reaching effects—it seems that the beach will become part of elephant seal territory going forward.

MARINE MAMMAL CENTER

The Marine Mammal Center in Sausalito, California, just north of San Francisco, is a working wildlife hospital and rehabilitation center. You can see all types of seals here, including northern elephant seals.

Staff at the center feed, handle, house and help with disease and stress prevention while animals are in care. The goal is to release the creatures back into the wild when they are well enough with their natural abilities and instincts intact. This means that maintaining the wildness of the animals is an important part of the work the center does. It's a tall order! The animals are handled just enough to treat them and make them better, all the while respecting and even nurturing their wildness.

Workers treat such pinnipeds as California sea lions, northern elephant seals and harbor seals, as well as sea otters, whales, dolphins, porpoises and sea turtles. Animals usually end up at the center because of malnutrition due to shifts in the ocean food chain or because they became separated from their mothers before weaning. Animals are also treated for such things as toxic algae poisoning, bacterial infections, skin disease and injuries from such things as gunshots, shark bites and getting hit by boats or caught in ocean trash. It's a dangerous world out there, but as many as 600 injured marine mammals are cared for by the center's staff and volunteers every year.

RACE ROCKS

A new, small colony has been established at Race Rocks Ecological Reserve in the Juan de Fuca Strait, which lies between British Columbia and Washington State. At the time I am writing this book, the population of seals at this colony is less than 20. Elephant seals have been spotted at Race Rocks for around ten years, with the first documented birth being January 30, 2009. Each year just a few more seals haul out and a few more pups are born here. Researchers think this may be changing, though, and that these early regular visitors might be the first of many, as ocean temperatures continue to rise.

The newest elephant seal rookery is at Race Rocks in British Columbia. Researchers think that as the oceans warm, we might see more members of this highly adaptive species heading north to Race Rocks. BIRDIEGAL717/DREAMSTIME.COM

The beach at Coos Bay, Oregon.
MIKE BRAKE/DREAMSTIME.COM

ALONG THE COAST

While the most established rookeries have historically been in Mexico and California, in recent years seals have established small colonies at Coos Bay in Oregon and, as previously mentioned, at Race Rocks in British Columbia. Occasionally an adult will haul out to molt on their own at some unexpected place, such as the female who created a stir at Gonzales Beach in Victoria, British Columbia, in 2018. People called various animal resources to report the sick seal on the beach. She wasn't sick at all, though, just going through her annual catastrophic molt. After about a month she pulled up stakes and slipped back into the sea.

If you ever happen upon a seal on some lonely beach, leave it alone. They look gentle—and mostly they are— but they are also wild animals. They do not eat humans, but they could do some damage if they felt threatened. Keep a respectful distance and examine them only with your eyes!

LINDA L. RICHARDS

ENVIRONMENTAL CHALLENGES

The elephant seal has shown itself to be capable of facing incredible challenges and coming out on top. Hunted to near extinction, northern elephant seals still managed a recovery that has possibly never been equaled. Part

It's especially important for moms to be well fed by the time they get back to their home beach, because it takes a lot of fatty milk to get those babies as big as they need to be before they are left to fend for themselves.
LINDA L. RICHARDS

of the way they did that is by being able to respond to changes in their environment quickly—creating mainland breeding grounds for possibly the first time in the twentieth century, for instance, when historically their rookeries had been on islands.

The seals' ability to adapt goes beyond choosing new locations for their colonies. Researchers have recently discovered that the way in which adult male northern elephant seals communicate is different than it was 50 years ago. Their language has changed! They used to have regional dialects. Think about the way someone speaks if they are from Texas versus the way someone speaks if they're from London, England. In both cases English is being spoken, but certain words and sounds are different.

It was like that with elephant seals too. Fifty years ago, if one male approached and uttered sounds, all of the other seals would be able to tell which rookery he was from. But the population recovered quickly and soon there were a lot more seals and rookeries. Where each seal was from became less important: more complex language was needed in order to convey additional information. It wasn't just Ben from Guadalupe Island or Sam from Año Nuevo anymore. Now it was Christopher or Benjamin, Alexander and Sebastian. There are now more syllables in their communications with each other, but the way they vocalize isn't connected to where they are from, possibly because—with so many more seals around—where they are from is no longer as important as who they are as individuals. Each "voice" holds much more information for the seal that is listening, making it possible for competitive seals to know just who they are dealing with before risking an encounter.

CLIMATE CHANGE

In the coming years environmental factors will likely put more pressure on elephant seal populations to adapt in order to thrive. Rising sea temperatures, changes in the quality and quantity of available food and other factors might impact the northern elephant seal in ways we can't even imagine right now.

For example, scientists have noted that the male-to-female ratio of elephant seal births is affected by climatic conditions. When the climate is warmer, more males than females are born. This might be an adaptation that takes into account the foraging and hunting patterns of both genders. If, for example, less food will be available where the females generally forage, it's an advantage to the species for there to be fewer of them foraging for the food available. A species' ability to survive such variables as El Niño can determine that species' long-term success.

EL NIÑO

El Niño is the term for a natural event that takes place every three to five years when the temperature of the water near the surface of the tropical Pacific Ocean rises.

When an El Niño occurs, the trade winds have weakened in the central and western parts of the Pacific Ocean. That makes the surface temperature of the water warm up, causing the release of energy into the atmosphere to a degree so great it causes weather changes everywhere on Earth.

There have always been El Niños. Climate records show El Niños occurring millions of years ago. They can be dated by their effects on the rings of trees, the mud deep in the sea, coral, ice cores and other places where temperature changes leave a signature over time.

Since elephant seals have been protected from human intervention, their numbers have increased every single year—with one exception. In years when El Niño battered the west coast, many pups who were still too young to be on their own were swept out to sea. Most of them perished because they were just too little to fend for themselves. In those years, the elephant seal population did not increase.

GENETIC CHALLENGES

Whenever northern elephant seals are written about or discussed, you inevitably hear the word *bottleneck*. What does that mean?

A genetic bottleneck is created when some catastrophe, such as fire, famine, disease or human activities, kills off a large percentage of the population of a species. The available gene pool is made much smaller. This can be a problem because research has shown that the larger the pool of genes available, the healthier an overall population will be. With a smaller gene pool, negative traits will be enlarged from generation to generation.

When you think about you and your friends, there is probably a lot of variation in how you all look. Some friends have dark skin and some have light. Some of your friends have red hair and some have black or brown or blond. Taller, shorter, thinner, thicker—the genetic material available to North American humans now means that even if all your friends were ethnically the same as you, it would be unlikely that any of them were related to you.

LINDA L. RICHARDS

Because the population of northern elephant seals was so reduced between 1850 and 1900, it's not hard to see that the opposite is true. If you began with 100 individuals at most and now there are well over 200,000, everyone is related.

This creates some challenges. For example, if one of those original 100 animals had a genetic disorder, that disorder would now have been passed on to the whole population because all the animals are related. Not only that, but because that gene was amplified by generations of inbreeding, it's possible that this genetic disorder could become the norm for the whole population.

77

SINGLE VOICES MAKING A DIFFERENCE

The fact is, when people stand together for something they believe in, they *can* make a difference. I think about those good people in the Mexican government in 1922 saying, "No! No more! The hunting of elephant seals must stop." In the end they protected—and ultimately saved—a whole species. Imagine!

Former NBA basketball star Yao Ming used his influence to tell a whole nation not to eat shark fin soup, a delicacy that has contributed to making many shark species endangered. The result? In a 10-year period consumption of shark fin soup had dropped by *82 percent*. That saved millions of sharks every year and maybe saved the entire species.

Okay, fair enough. We're not all international basketball stars, but change starts with one little word.

But that is not how it is has played out for the northern elephant seal. In 2012 the Marine Mammal Center reported that of the 3,000 elephant seals that received care at the center between 1975 and 2012, 1 percent of them had birth defects. The defects were of the type usually associated with interbreeding, with cleft palates and humped backs being the two leading deformities. In cases such as these, the center does not interfere, letting nature take its course. Staff say they have seen animals with these specific deformities lead completely normal elephant seal lives.

Dr. Bill Van Bonn, former director of veterinary sciences at the Marine Mammal Center and now vice-president of animal health at the Shedd Aquarium in Chicago, thinks the genetic bottleneck in elephant seals will eventually solve itself. "Science leads us to expect that over time, these seals will 're-evolve' and these problems will become less and less," he says. "But that could take thousands of years."

Scientists are still not sure what the long-term effects of such a tiny gene pool will be. They are monitoring the situation closely and have reasons (scientific ones!) to be optimistic. After all, for the most part, the elephant seal population is really thriving and their geographic ranges are getting bigger. Both of those facts indicate good things ahead for the northern elephant seal.

In a successful campaign for WildAid, international basketball star Yao Ming pushes his shark fin soup away. "When the buying stops, the killing does too." WILDAID.ORG

The super cute and very tiny island fox is the least genetically diverse animal on the planet. It shares some of the same challenges that the elephant seal is facing due to a narrow gene pool.

NEIGHBORS WITH A NARROW GENE POOL

The award for tiniest gene pool in the world goes to the island fox, native to six of the Channel Islands off California. Previously endangered, they are *super* cute. Each one is only 4 to 6.5 inches (10 to 16.5 centimeters) tall and weighs 2 to 6 pounds (0.9 to 2.7 kilograms), which is smaller than your average house cat. The fox's tiny size is thought to be an adaptation to the limited space and resources available in an island environment. There are actually six subspecies of island fox. Each subspecies is native to a specific Channel Island. It is because of this island evolution that the fox's gene pool is so small. On Santa Catalina Island in 2000, as few as 100 native foxes were left as a result of predation and disease. Thanks to conservation efforts, there are now more than 1,500.

Help protect our wildlife!
LINDA L. RICHARDS

A GOOD-NEWS STORY

I am once again standing on the boardwalk at Piedras Blancas. It feels like coming home.

It is pupping season. And it's a calm year—there will be no El Niño.

I walk along the boardwalk slowly, stopping frequently. Sometimes I take photographs. Sometimes I just observe.

The surf. The wind against the rocks. Black-furred babies nursing or screeching at their dams. Anxious males jockeying for position, hollering at each other, then collapsing into tired heaps. Vultures and gulls strutting along the shore, pecking at anonymous pup-sized lumps in the sand. Older pups crowding together for companionship and games.

Females jealously guarding their precious fuzzy-furred bundles until the time comes when they will abandon them on the beach and go off in search of a meal. It's the circle of life, perfectly rendered on this beach. A complete society, right down to friendships and disagreements. An animal society that could so easily not have been.

I stand here watching the gentle drama, and I think also about how you and I ended up having this conversation. My journey with the northern elephant seal came about because I stumbled on a good-news story that was not well known, and I wanted to share it with you.

The northern elephant seal is a big success story. And now you know about it. And maybe together we can create even more good news, even more success. Let's work toward that. Together.

There's always action in the rookery. Elephant seals are very social at the beach, calling to one another, playing, fighting for dominance, and often snuggling quite close while they snooze.
LINDA L. RICHARDS

GLOSSARY

Note: Some of these words have several meanings. The definitions here are specific to how the words are used in this book.

adaptation—how a species evolves to be better suited to its current surroundings and situations

afterbirth—the placenta and fetal membranes discharged from the uterus after a mother gives birth

apex predator—a predator at the top of the food chain who has few natural predators; a top-level predator

beachmaster—an alpha male elephant seal, fully mature and seasoned enough in battle to have proven himself to other males, earning him the right to breed with females and be the father of baby elephant seals

the bends—another name for decompression sickness, which occurs when there is a rapid decrease in the pressure surrounding a person or animal, which results in gases such as nitrogen bubbling up inside the body's tissues; an example is when a scuba diver surfaces from deep in the ocean too quickly

bioaccumulates—becomes concentrated in a living organism over time, for example, the gradual accumulation of substances such as mercury, pesticides and chemicals in an animal's body

bioluminescent—emitting light as the result of an internal chemical reaction within a living organism's body

blubber—the thick layer of fat found under the skin of all cetaceans (whales), pinnipeds (seals) and sirenians (sea cows like manatees)

bottleneck—an area where something wide narrows like the neck of a bottle and traffic going through it is impeded by the narrowness; a genetic bottleneck happens when a population's gene pool is drastically reduced

bull—an adult male

catastrophic molt—the shedding of skin and/or hair in order to accommodate new growth

chest shield—the scarred and callused skin that develops on the chest of adult male elephant seals

colony—a place on land where elephant seals congregate to mate, give birth and molt; also known as a *rookery*

continental shelf—the area of seabed around a large land mass, important because it is much less deep here than in the rest of the ocean

docents—teachers or guides

epoch—a period of time in history marked by distinctive features or key developments

Great Pacific Garbage Patch—a floating mass of plastic, chemical sludge and other garbage, also known as the Pacific trash vortex, that extends over a large area halfway between Hawaii and California

harem—a group of female animals who share the same male mate

haul-out—the unofficial term for elephant seals' leaving the ocean and coming onto land;

the term comes from the nautical practice of taking a boat out of the water annually to examine and repair it

nictitating membrane—the transparent protective third eyelid in reptiles, birds and some mammals

oxidation—a change to a chemical substance when oxygen is added

pinnipeds—fin-footed, semiaquatic animals, including seals and walruses

proboscis—the long and flexible nose of an animal

rookery—a place on land where elephant seals congregate to mate, give birth and molt; also called *colony*

rudder—the part of the steering system on a boat that is underneath the water

sexually dimorphic—the condition where the male and female of a species are visibly different in size and/or coloring

subsidies—financial incentives, usually from government, to support a desired outcome

talismans—objects thought to have magical powers or to bring good luck

top-level predator—a predator at the top of the food chain who has few natural predators; an apex predator

try pot—a large pot, usually cast iron, used to render the oil from blubber obtained from whales, penguins and seals

RESOURCES

PRINT

Adams, Carole and Phil. *Elephant Seals*. San Luis Obispo, CA: Central Coast Books, 1999.

Haug, Elisabeth. *California Elephant Seals*. Self-published, Sharing Magic Moments, 2014.

Laws, Richard M., and Burney J. Le Boeuf, eds. *Elephant Seals: Population Ecology, Behavior, and Physiology*. Oakland, CA: University of California Press, 1994.

Leiren-Young, Mark. *Orcas Everywhere: The Mystery and History of Killer Whales*. Victoria, BC: Orca Book Publishers, 2019.

Read, Nicholas. *The Seal Garden*. Victoria, BC: Orca Book Publishers, 2018.

Robinson, Patrick, and Roxanne Beltran. *A Seal Named Patches*. Fairbanks, AK: University of Alaska Press, 2017.

Stille, Darlene R. *I Am a Seal: The Life of an Elephant Seal*. North Mankato, MN: Capstone Books, 2004.

ONLINE

Adopt an elephant seal at the World Wildlife Fund: gifts.worldwildlife.org/
gift-center/gifts/Species-Adoptions/Elephant-Seal.aspx

Año Nuevo Natural Reserve: anonuevoreserve.ucsc.edu

Año Nuevo Island live cam: parks.ca.gov/live/anonuevoisland

The Costa Lab: costa.eeb.ucsc.edu

Elephant Seal Research Group: eleseal.org

Friends of the Elephant Seal: elephantseal.org

Institute of Marine Sciences at the University of California, Santa Cruz:
ims-new.ucsc.edu/news-events/news/index.html

The Marine Mammal Center: marinemammalcenter.org

National Geographic Elephant Seals page: nationalgeographic.com/
animals/mammals/group/elephant-seals

Northern elephant seal tracking: seaturtle.org/tracking/?project_id=1273

Piedras Blancas Northern Elephant Seal Research Facebook page:
facebook.com/PBElephantSeals

TEDx talk by Dr. Dan Costa: youtube.com/
watch?time_continue=29&v=4IbSp9Ha_zs

ACKNOWLEDGMENTS

One of the interesting things about doing research is discovering how much we, as humans, don't know about so many things, even though we sometimes act like we know it all!

In this book you will encounter the phrases "as far as we know" and the word "might" more often than I'd like. This is because either the experts don't agree or not enough work has been done in that particular area for me to relay the response with confidence.

While the amount we don't know about a lot of things is astonishing, it's also exciting. There are so many answers out there just waiting to be found. You and I might find answers no one else has. Imagine! So many discoveries still waiting to be made.

I tried very hard to get everything in this book right, but conclusive answers weren't always possible. I did my best, and if I got things right, it is in part because of the work done by a handful of hardworking researchers and passionate volunteers, all of whom seem to really love the special creatures we focus on in this book. The things that are right, are right because of them. And if I got anything wrong, it is my fault entirely.

One of the people who gets so many things right is Dr. Patrick W. Robinson, director of Año Nuevo Natural Reserve and lecturer at the University of California, Santa Cruz. He carved out time for me in his stunning lab, volunteered information and answered questions when I hit a wall. He's also a terrifically gifted and committed man who I am happy to know is looking out for the future of the elephant seal.

Dr. Daniel Costa is a distinguished professor of Ecology and Evolutionary Biology at the University of California, Santa Cruz and has made important contributions to contemporary knowledge on the northern elephant seal and other seagoing species. He was also very generous with his time and patient with my questions.

The Friends of the Elephant Seal is based in historic San Simeon, California, close to Piedras Blancas, the largest modern elephant seal rookery. It is a fantastic resource for people interested in elephant seals and for the seals themselves. The organization puts a lot of energy into helping thousands of people every year learn more about this fascinating species.

Thanks to my editor at Orca Book Publishers, the wonderful Kirstie Hudson, who owns this amazing blend of enthusiasm and virtuosity in her field that makes her a delight to work with. Energy and talent run deeply through the whole organization at Orca—I feel very blessed to be a small part of their team.

Thanks also to my husband, Tony, my son, Mike, and my brother, Peter, for their constant support and unshakable belief in me and the seals.

INDEX

*Page numbers in **bold** indicate an image caption.*

activists
  ocean garbage, 63–65
  shark protection, 78
adaptations, 82
  eyesight, 15–16
  hearing, 8, 16, 18
  to ocean warming, 65, 76
  oxygen storage, 12, 13, 26, 58
  and swimming, 11, **48**
  water retention, 60
ancestors, 25–28
Año Nuevo, CA, 85
  guided tours, 68–69
  rookery, **14**, **17**, **40**, **55**, 67
Antarctica, **9**
apex predator, 55, 82
appearance
  males, **4**, **41**, 62
  pups, **7**, **14**, **36**, 43
  size, **6**, 15, **18**, 83

Barnhart, Diana, 15
beachmaster, 18, 20, **22**, 82
bears, 25, **26**, 37, 39
behaviors
  fasting period, 54, 59–60
  feeding, 10–13, 53–54
  migrations, 9–10, 43–46, **52**, 67
  play-fighting, **3**, **20**, **55**, 61
  pupping season, 22, 40, 80–81
  on the sand, 49, **50**, 60
  social, **2**, **46**, **81**
  vocalizations, 7, 8, 21–22, 74, **75**
  yearly cycle, 23
Big Sur, CA, 1, 2, 67
bioaccumulates, 51, 82
bioluminescent, 15, 82
blubber, 20, 82
  oil extraction, 29, 31
bottleneck, genetic, 77–78, 79, 82
breathing, 11–13, 26
British Columbia, rookery sites,
  19, 72
bulls, 10, 82
  See also males

California
  commercial hunting, 33
  ecotourism, 68–72
  grizzly bears, 37
  rookery sites, **19**, 40–41

Canada, 36
captivity, **10**
catastrophic molt, **36**, 43, 46,
  47–50, 51, 82
Cedros Island, Mexico, 32, 40
Channel Islands, CA, **10**, 36, 40, 79
characteristics
  ears, 16, 18
  eyes, 15–16
  molt, **36**, 43, 46, 47–50, 51, 82
  nostrils, 11–12
  skull, **26**
  and small gene pool, 77–78
  species, 9–10
  See also adaptations
chest shield, 20–21, 22, 82
climate change
  impact of, 72–74, 76
  ocean warming, 65, 72
colony, 18, 82
  See also rookery sites
commercial hunting, 29–36
communication
  baby seal sound, 7
  complex, 74, **75**
  loudness of, 5, 7, 8, **42**
  and territory, 21–22
cookiecutter sharks, 56
Coos Bay, OR, 73
Costa, Daniel, 67, 68, 85

diet
  fish, 15–16, 51, 53
  and mercury, 51, 82
  squids and octopuses, 51, 53, 55
  and water retention, 60
diving, 10, 11–13, 26, 58, 68
docents, 3, 71, 82
ducks, **15**

ecotourism, 68–72
electronic tags, 67
elephants, 5, 10, 27
Elephant Seal Monitoring Project,
  66
elephant seals
  drawings of, **24**, **32**, **33**
  species, 9–10, 25–28
  terminology, 10, 56
El Niño, 76
environmental factors

climate change, 65, 72, 76
  garbage, 63–65
  new rookery sites, 73–74
extinct species, recreating, 37
eyesight, 15–16

fasting period, 54, 59–60
females
  birth rate of, 76
  care of pups, **7**, 23, 43–45
  delayed implantation, 44, 45
  feeding patterns, 53–54
  health of, **74**
  mating, **17**, 18
  migrations, 43–45, **52**
  size of, 15
  weight loss, 43, 59
fish, 15–16, 51, 53
fishing nets, 63, 65
foxes, 79
fuel oils, 29–33
fur seals, 56, **57**

garbage, 63–65
gender differences
  birth rate, 76
  migrations, 43–46, **52**
  size, 15
genetic bottleneck, 77–78, 79, 82
Goliath (elephant seal), **10**
Great Pacific Garbage Patch, 65, 82
Guadalupe Island, Mexico, **13**, 32,
  33, 34, 36, 40, 41

habitat. See rookery sites
harbor seals, 11, **57**
harem, 18, 82
haul-out, 46, 82
health concerns
  bioaccumulation, 51
  for females, 74
  genetic bottleneck, 77–78
hearing, 8, 16, 18
human–elephant seal interactions,
  55, 73
hunting
  diet, 53–54, 55
  diving, 10, 11–13, 26, 58, 68
  eyesight, 15–16
  migrations, 43–46, **52**, 67
  speed, 11

Indigenous people, 28–29

language. *See* vocalizations
Lord of the Rings (film), 7

males
  chest shield, 20–21, 22, 82
  feeding patterns, 53–54
  mating, 7, **17**, 18, 20–23
  migrations, 45, **52**
  play-fighting, **3**, **20**, **55**, 61
  proboscis, **4**, 5, **6**, 7, 10, 83
  size of, 9–10, 15, **18**
  vocalizations, 7, 8
  weight loss, 59
mallard ducks, **15**
marine life
  mammals, 29–32
  pinnipeds, 11, 25–28, 29, 45,
    56, **57**, 83
  threats to, 63, 65
Marine Mammal Center, CA,
  71–72, 78
mating
  behaviors, 7, **17**, 18, 20–23
  delayed implantation, 44, 45
mercury, 48, 51
Mexico
  and protected species status,
    34, 36
  rookery sites, **19**, 40–41
migrations
  range, 9–10, **52**, 67
  yearly cycle, 43–46
Ming, Yao, 78
molting. *See* catastrophic molt
museum collectors, 34, 35

northern elephant seals
  populations, 3, 36, 39, 68, 76
  range of, 9, **52**, 67
  rookery sites map, **19**

Ocean Cleanup, 63–65
oceans
  El Niño, 76
  floating garbage, 63–65
  warming of, 65, 72
Ocean Voyages Institute, 63
oil industry, 29–33
Oligocene epoch, 26, 27
orcas, 13, 45, 53, 61
Oregon, rookery sites, **19**, 73
oxygen storage, 12, 13, 26, 58

penguins, 9, 29, 47

Piedras Blancas, CA
  about, 2–3, 46, 67, 69, 85
  pupping season, 40, 80–81
  rookery, **ii**, **vi**, **38**, **53**, **61**
pinnipeds
  characteristics, 11, 45, 56, **57**, 83
  hunting of, 29
  origins, 25–28
Point Reyes National Seashore, CA,
  62, 66, 70, 71
pollution
  mercury, 51
  plastic, 63–64
populations
  genetic bottleneck, 77–78
  growth of, 3, 36, 39, 68, 76
predators
  land, **37**, 39, 40
  orcas, 13, 45, 53, 61
  sharks, 13, **38**, 45, 56, 61
  and sleep, 13
prey. *See* diet
proboscis, **4**, 5, **6**, 7, 10, 83
pups and juveniles, **14**, **35**, **39**
  care of, **7**, 23, 43–45
  skills learning, 3, **13**, 23, 45–46,
    61
  sounds, 7
  survival rate, 76
  terminology, 10

Race Rocks, Vancouver Island, BC,
  65, 72
rehabilitation centers, 71–72
reproduction
  care of pups, **7**, 23, 43–45
  delayed implantation, 44, 45
  female pups, 76
  mating, 7, **17**, 18, 20–23
Robinson, Patrick W., 65, 84
rookery sites
  characteristics, 61, 83
  commercial hunting, 32–33
  ecotourism, 68–72
  expansion of, 3, 65, 71, 73
  map, **19**
  modern, 39–41
  and ocean warming, 65, 72
  yearly cycle, 23, 46, 80–81

San Benito Island, Mexico, 40, 41
San Miguel Island, CA, 36, 67
San Nicolas Island, CA, 66, 67
Scammon, Charles, 33
schools, data collection, 66
scientific research

data collection, 34–36, 65–67
  early, 29, 32–33
  and extinct species, 37
  genetic bottleneck, 77–78
  resources for, 84, 85
  tagging, **47**, 66, 67
sea lions, 11, 56
sea monsters, **24**, 25
sexually dimorphic, 15, 83
shark fin soup, 78
sharks, 13, **38**, 45, 53, 61
  cookiecutter, 56
  protection of, 78
Sir Francis Drake High School,
  San Anselmo, CA, 66
skin
  human, 47
  molting, **36**, 43, 47–50
Slat, Boyan, 64
sleeping, 12, 13
Smithsonian Institution, 34, 35
social organization
  at rookery, 20–23, 80–81
  and solitary lives, 12, **46**
sounds. *See* vocalizations
southern elephant seals, 9–10, **30**
South Georgia Island, **30**
species
  classification, 25–28
  differences, 9–10
spleen function, 58
squids and octopuses, 51, 53, 55

tagging, **47**, 66, 67
top-level predator, 48, 55, 83

United States, **19**, 36

Vancouver Island, BC, 65, 72
Victoria, BC, 73
vocalizations, **42**
  of baby seals, 7
  complex, 74, **75**
  loudness of, 5, 7, 8
  and territory, 21–22

walruses, 11, 56, **57**
whales, 25, 31, 68
whaling industry, 29, **30**, 31
wildlife
  and humans, 55, 73
  rescue, **47**, 71–72
Wing, Michael, 66

zoos, **10**

JEANNIE LEE

LINDA L. RICHARDS is a journalist, editor and award-winning author. She is the founding editor of *January Magazine*, one of the Web's most respected voices about books. Linda divides her time between Vancouver, Phoenix and Paso Robles, California.